HAWK HEAVEN

THE ROAD TO THE SEAHAWKS' FIRST SUPER BOWL VICTORY

Super Bowl XLVIII
Champions

The Seattle Times

The Seattle Times

SEATTLETIMES.COM

Sports Editor: Don Shelton
Book Editor: Ed Guzman
Photo Editors: Danny Gawlowski, Fred Nelson, Angela Gottschalk
Lead Designer: Rich Boudet
Copy Editor: Scott Hanson
Reporters: Jerry Brewer, Larry Stone, Bob Condotta, Jayson Jenks, Jack Broom
Photographers: John Lok, Dean Rutz, Bettina Hansen, Ellen M. Banner, Lindsey Wasson,
Mike Siegel, Genevieve Alvarez
Photo Production: Heather Trimm
Illustrator: David Miller
Editorial Project Manager: Denise Clifton
News Business Development Manager: Denise Lee

Front cover photo: John Lok
Back cover photo: Mike Siegel

Peter J. Clark, Publisher
Molly Voorheis, Managing Editor
Katherine Grigsby, Layout & Design

ISBN: 978-1-940056-06-7 (PB)
ISBN: 978-1-940056-09-8 (HC)

Printed in the United States of America
KCI Sports Publishing   3340 Whiting Avenue, Suite 5   Stevens Point, WI 54481
Phone: 1-800-697-3756   Fax: 715-344-2668
www.kcisports.com

CONTENTS

The celebration was underway in MetLife Stadium after the Seahawks beat the Broncos, 43-8, in Super Bowl XLVIII to secure Seattle's first NFL championship.

By Mike Siegel / The Seattle Times

True grit

Seahawks were ready for this glorious moment

By JERRY BREWER | *Seattle Times columnist*

The dream actually began amid despair. Rewind back to Jan. 13, 2013, the day the Seahawks lost a heartbreaking playoff game in Atlanta.

They rallied from a 20-point fourth quarter deficit, took the lead with 31 seconds remaining — and blew the game. But as the team trudged off the Georgia Dome field that day, with a 30-28 loss to the Atlanta Falcons, Russell Wilson, then a rookie quarterback, looked at quarterbacks coach Carl Smith and declared: "I'm so excited. I can't wait to get to the offseason and work and work and work."

That's where the anticipation for the 2013 season began, in a tear-soaked locker room overcome by child-like enthusiasm. The Seahawks were no longer young and aloof. They had experienced a meteoric rise and learned a valuable postseason lesson. They were ready to handle what came next.

They were ready to win a championship.

In the most glorious season in Seattle sports history, the Seahawks followed through with their intentions, rumbling through a 13-3 regular season and winning three postseason matchups, including a stunning 43-8 blowout of Denver in Super Bowl XLVIII. To win their first championship, the Seahawks had to beat two former Super Bowl-winning quarterbacks, Drew Brees and Peyton Manning. They had to beat their evil twin, the San Francisco 49ers. But most of all, they had to outlast the unprecedented hype they faced from the moment the 2012 season ended in Atlanta.

The Seahawks did it with the best defense in the NFL, becoming the first team since the 1985 Chicago Bears to lead the league in total defense, scoring defense and takeaways. They did it with a secondary nicknamed the Legion of Boom, a dominant unit featuring three All-Pro defensive backs (Earl Thomas, Richard Sherman and Kam Chancellor) that defied the notion that the best defenses are built front to back. They did it with running back Marshawn Lynch running over defenders and Wilson dancing around them and receivers Golden Tate and Doug Baldwin jumping over them.

The Seahawks' way is the finest example in the

Seahawks coach Pete Carroll, embracing Doug Baldwin during the Super Bowl, preached competition and declared every game a championship opportunity.

By Bettina Hansen / The Seattle Times

NFL now. The rest of the league will attempt to rob from their formula, which is as unorthodox as it gets. In a league currently obsessed with scoring points and throwing the football, the Seahawks are a throwback, with their ground-and-pound style. They built what was widely hailed as the league's deepest roster by finding overlooked talent — late-round draft gems, undrafted free agents, reclamation projects — and putting them in the best positions to showcase what they can do, ignoring their perceived limitations. They were willing to try anything: a 323-pound defensive end, a 6-foot-3 cornerback, a 5-foot-11 quarterback.

The 2013 Seahawks were so complete a team that they managed without their prized offseason acquisition, wide receiver Percy Harvin, who only played 30 snaps over two games until the Super Bowl. Coach Pete Carroll preaches competition and alters the "one game at a time" cliché by declaring that every game is a championship opportunity. The Seahawks took it as gospel, and despite considerable reshuffling because

of injuries, they lost only three games by a total of 15 points.

"I think what makes us special is that we are a very, very tight group," Carroll said. "We have a very team-oriented makeup. Our locker room is really connected. Our guys really care for one another. They play for each other. I think we have a well-balanced football team that allows them to express themselves."

They're bonded by their grit. That's what Carroll and general manager John Schneider wanted when they put this team together – grit. A team that refuses to give an inch on anything. A team that is obsessed with pushing its own boundaries rather than simply being good enough to beat the competition.

In their locker room, the Seahawks posted signs that read "Seahawks 24/7, Leave No Doubt." They didn't talk much about winning a Super Bowl. They focused on winning the NFC West and maximizing every moment they had together.

The result was a 19-game masterpiece, the best season in franchise history, a championship season.

Seattle owns a Lombardi Trophy now. And with one of the youngest teams in the NFL, there's a good chance this won't be the Seahawks' last.

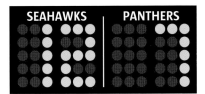

SEAHAWKS | PANTHERS

REGULAR SEASON
> GAME 1

Sept. 8, 2013
SEAHAWKS @
PANTHERS

THE WINNING HIT

Hawks force late fumble to seal tight victory over Panthers

By **BOB CONDOTTA** | *Seattle Times staff reporter*

The Seahawks locker room had largely cleared out after Seattle's season-opening 12-7 win over Carolina.

As is custom, though, two who still remained were cornerback Richard Sherman and safety Earl Thomas.

And as Thomas heard Sherman talk to a reporter about the game's key play — a fumble by Carolina's DeAngelo Williams with just over five minutes left in the fourth quarter that the Seahawks recovered at the Seattle 8 — he playfully interrupted.

"Don't go taking my credit, now," Thomas said. "I'm listening over here."

"OK," Sherman eventually decided. "Can we have half-and-half?"

Officially, it was Thomas who got credit for causing the fumble on a play when both Seattle defenders hit Williams as the Panthers appeared to be on the verge of a go-ahead score.

Ultimately, though, all they really cared about

Player Of The Game

It didn't always go smoothly for Russell Wilson, but when the game ended he had thrown for a career-high 320 yards in helping the Seahawks overcome a sluggish running game. Wilson hit on 24 of his last 28 passes after a 1-for-5 start.

Earl Thomas had good reason to shout after he and Richard Sherman hit the Panthers' DeAngelo Williams, causing a fumble the Seahawks recovered at the Seattle 8-yard line late in the game.

By John Lok / The Seattle Times

was that the play happened, the kind of play the Seahawks say is indicative of what their team is all about.

"Great defenses find a way," Sherman said. "And that's what we try to do."

The fumble forced by Thomas and officially recovered by Tony McDaniel was one of two big plays turned in by the Seahawks in the fourth quarter that allowed them to begin their season of great expectations with something of a great escape.

For most of the afternoon in Charlotte, N.C., it was a real slog as the Seahawks struggled to get a running game going or protect quarterback Russell Wilson. And they were just vulnerable enough on defense to give up one long touchdown drive in the second quarter.

That combination had Seattle staring at a 7-6 deficit as it began its first drive of the fourth quarter.

A Golden Tate 11-yard reception on third down, though, followed by a 15-yard run by Robert Turbin got the Seahawks to the Carolina 43-yard line.

Once there, the Seahawks noticed that the Panthers were getting a little more aggressive in their coverage, and on first down Wilson threw deep to Stephen Williams, who was open down the sideline. The pass was just a little long and went through the hands of a diving Williams for what momentarily looked like a lost opportunity.

Game statistics

Seattle ....0 3 3 6 — 12
Carolina ....0 7 0 0 — 7

SECOND QUARTER

Sea—Hauschka 27 FG, 9:36.
Drive: 15 plays, 74 yards, 8:47.

Car—Smith 3 pass from
Newton (Gano kick), 3:13.
Drive: 11 plays, 80 yards, 6:23.

THIRD QUARTER

Sea—Hauschka 40 FG, 2:22.
Drive: 9 plays, 43 yards, 4:14.

FOURTH QUARTER

Sea—Kearse 43 pass from
Wilson (pass failed), 10:13.
Drive: 6 plays, 74 yards, 2:45.

Attendance: 73,294.

NET YARDS GAINED

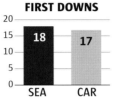

| | SEA CAR | SEA CAR |
| | *Passing yards* | *Rushing yards* |

FIRST DOWNS

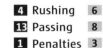

| SEA | CAR |
| 18 | 17 |

TIME OF POSSESSION

29:46 CAR   30:14 SEA

4	Rushing	**6**
13	Passing	**8**
1	Penalties	**3**

Seahawks quarterback Russell Wilson had his highest passing-yardage day of the regular season against the Panthers, the first of many notable performances for Wilson.

By John Lok / The Seattle Times

No matter. On second down, the Seahawks tried a similar play, this time with Jermaine Kearse in place of Williams.

Kearse said he noticed Carolina cornerback Josh Thomas creeping up to the line of scrimmage to play tight coverage. So Kearse, given an option of routes on the play depending on what he saw out of the defender, ran a go route down the sideline.

This time, Wilson's pass was on target. Kearse grabbed it between Thomas and closing safety Charles Godfrey for a touchdown to put Seattle ahead 12-7 with 10:13 left (a pass on the two-point conversion fell incomplete).

"It was a great catch," said Seahawks coach Pete Carroll. "It was a great throw. And it was cool to see the guys come through when we went right back after them."

It was the first regular-season touchdown for Kearse, the second-year player from Washington who made Seattle's roster in 2012 as an undrafted free agent.

"I looked at (Wilson) and saw him look my way," Kearse said, "And I seen him throw the ball and I knew there was a very good chance I could make that play — especially in the position I was in."

Said Wilson: "I just went through my progressions. He was my second read, to be honest with you."

Then came nervous time for the Seahawks as two 15-yard penalties helped Carolina move to the Seattle 24, where on second-and-two DeAngelo Williams took a handoff and burst free down the sideline before being hit by Sherman. Thomas, who had initially been beaten by Williams and was trailing the play, followed from behind and punched the ball out.

Each later gave credit to the endless practice sessions focused on forcing turnovers.

"He was doing a great job running hard, but he ran with it a little more loose and I tried to put my helmet and shoulder pads on it," Sherman said, "and right after he got by me, Earl put a fist on it. Day in, day out, that's all we practice, going after the ball."

Said Thomas: "You could see the ball and when (running backs) are swinging it and you see a little brown, you just want to punch, and I punched, and the ball came out and I just went crazy."

The Seattle offense then ran out the clock, capping what Carroll called "a great finish."

"It was hard today," Carroll said. "It was really hard. The thing I love about it is our guys hung tough and we made the plays when we needed to make them."

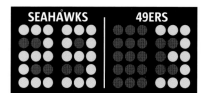

SEAHAWKS 49ERS

REGULAR SEASON
> GAME 2
Sept. 15, 2013
49ERS @
SEAHAWKS

LOUD AND CLEAR

Hawks get thunderous win over 49ers before record crowd

By BOB CONDOTTA | *Seattle Times staff reporter*

The waiting, it turns out, was the hardest part for the Seahawks.

And not just a one-hour delay after lightning near CenturyLink Field forced officials to stop the game for the safety of players and fans.

The Seahawks also couldn't wait for the game against San Francisco to arrive after listening to what they felt were a string of slights throughout the week leading up to it from pundits praising the 49ers and predicting doom for Seattle.

"A lot of things were said this week that we didn't really appreciate," said cornerback Richard Sherman, who helped lead a dominating defense that powered the Seahawks to a surprisingly easy 29-3 win over the 49ers in an early-season battle for supremacy in the NFC West, if not the NFC.

Reminded of some national pundits who picked against the Seahawks, Sherman responded with: "You see how smart they are? They must not have watched the last game we played them."

Richard Sherman came up with one of the Seahawks' three interceptions against the 49ers early in the fourth quarter, all but extinguishing San Francisco's hopes of getting back in the game.

By Dean Rutz / The Seattle Times

Player Of The Game

With the offense struggling, Marshawn Lynch emerged in the second half as a dual threat, scoring on a 14-yard run in the third quarter, a 7-yard reception early in the fourth quarter and a 2-yard run late in the game. Lynch finished the game with 98 yards rushing on 28 carries and 37 yards on three receptions.

Marshawn Lynch finished off this 7-yard touchdown reception by stopping at the goal line for a moment before tiptoeing into the end zone with no 49ers defender within reach.

By Dean Rutz / The Seattle Times

Game statistics

S. Francisco...0 0 3 0 — 3
Seattle ....0 5 7 17 — 29

SECOND QUARTER

Sea — Penalty on Miller enforced in end zone for a Safety, 10:39.

Sea — Hauschka 30 FG, 5:52. Drive: 6 plays, 17 yards, 2:15.

THIRD QUARTER

Sea — Lynch 14 run (Hauschka kick), 9:12. Drive: 10 plays, 80 yards, 5:48.

SF — Dawson 21 FG, 4:20. Drive: 9 plays, 71 yards, 4:52.

FOURTH QUARTER

Sea — Lynch 7 pass from Wilson (Hauschka kick), 13:44. Drive: 10 plays, 80 yards, 5:36.

Sea — Hauschka 37 FG, 11:31. Drive: 4 plays, 6 yards, 1:36.

Sea — Lynch 2 run (Hauschka kick), 4:22. Drive: 1 plays, 2 yards, 0:04.

Attendance: 68,338.

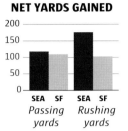

NET YARDS GAINED

FIRST DOWNS

SEA 19 SF 12

10	Rushing	**5**
5	Passing	**6**
4	Penalties	**1**

TIME OF POSSESSION

23:17 SF   36:43 SEA

That was a reference to Seattle's 42-13 home win over the 49ers in December 2012.

This one, in front of a crowd of 68,338 that was a record to witness a Seahawks game at CenturyLink, took a little longer.

It was tied at 0-0 when play was suspended with 3:13 left in the first quarter, fans uneasy both at the weather and some sluggish moments by the Seattle offense early.

The Seahawks, though, hardly seemed concerned — Sherman said he listened to music and danced with other members of the defense during the break.

And when play resumed, Seattle dominated.

Fittingly, the defense scored first, on a safety on a holding call early in the second quarter.

A field goal made it 5-0 at halftime, and in the locker room, Seattle figured that might be good enough.

"We knew we could win a game 5-0 because, playing our base stuff, they couldn't do anything against us," said Seahawks safety Earl Thomas. "That was just a great feeling to have."

The offense, though, got on track to begin the second half, going on 10-play, 80-yard drives each of the first two times it had the ball.

Marshawn Lynch capped each with touchdowns, the first a 14-yard run through the middle of the 49ers defense, the second a 7-yard pass from Russell Wilson. On the latter, he tiptoed into the end zone, literally stopping at the goal line for a second or two with no 49er defender within reach.

The second Lynch score made it 19-3 early in the fourth quarter and pretty much ended the drama in Seattle's ninth straight win at home.

And at that point, the game was in hand with Seattle's defense proving impenetrable, allowing only 207 yards and a lone field goal against a 49er team that had gained 494 yards and scored 34 points against Green Bay in its previous game.

"We did everything we needed to do on defense," said Seahawks coach Pete Carroll. "We had a great night on defense."

That included Sherman leading the effort to hold down San Francisco receiver Anquan Boldin to just one catch for 7yards.

Sherman said he asked to be allowed to guard Boldin as often as possible, straying from the usual

Cliff Avril and Seattle's defense smothered Colin Kaepernick and the 49ers' offense, forcing five turnovers.

By John Lok / The Seattle Times

Seattle tactic of leaving cornerbacks on their designated side regardless of where a receiver lines up.

Sherman had one of Seattle's three interceptions — fittingly, the other two were by Kam Chancellor and Thomas, meaning each of the three healthy Legion of Boom defenders (Brandon Browner was out with a hamstring injury) got a pick against San Francisco quarterback Colin Kaepernick.

Every stat gave evidence of Seattle's dominance.

A running game that was held to 70 yards against Carolina in Week 1 had 172 this time, with Lynch getting 98 on 28 attempts and scoring three touchdowns, two on the ground.

The 49ers, meanwhile, had just 100.

And Seattle held the ball for 36 minutes and 43 seconds, including 31:30 in the final three quarters.

A crowd that appeared to return en masse after the hourlong break loved every minute of it, breaking a Guinness record for stadium noise.

Carroll had no trouble believing the mark was broken, saying he had never heard it as loud and beginning his postgame comments by saying, "What an amazing night."

Amazing, maybe, but none of it was a surprise to the Seahawks, even if it might have been to others.

"Did we lose?" asked Sherman after being asked again about some of the pundits who picked the 49ers. "We did what we expected to do."

The fans at CenturyLink made themselves heard against the 49ers, setting a record for stadium crowd noise. The noise reached 136.6 decibels, a record the fans broke later in the season.

By Bettina Hansen / The Seattle Times

Doug Baldwin had his first touchdown reception of the season on this 35-yard pass from backup quarterback Tarvaris Jackson late in the third quarter.

By Dean Rutz / The Seattle Times

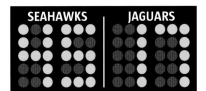

SEAHAWKS   JAGUARS

REGULAR SEASON
> GAME 3

Sept. 22, 2013
JAGUARS @
SEAHAWKS

TOP OF THE WORLD

Rest of the NFC West falters as Seahawks romp

By BOB CONDOTTA | *Seattle Times staff reporter*

A day that began with wind and rain at CenturyLink Field ended with clear skies and sunshine.

A good day, ultimately, to look around and enjoy the scenery.

Seahawks safety Earl Thomas, though, had trouble taking his eyes off the scoreboards, especially the ones showing the results of the other teams in the NFC West.

And what did Thomas see?

"L's," he said, meaning losses. "Trust me, I was looking. Especially after they took me out of the game, I started looking at the scores. I seen San Francisco lose. I was excited about that."

Indeed, Seattle's expected, and at times perfunctory-feeling, 45-17 victory over the Jacksonville Jaguars, combined with losses by the 49ers, Rams and Cardinals, left the Seahawks with an early commanding lead over the rest of the division.

Seattle is 3-0 while the other three teams are 1-2, giving the Seahawks a big early cushion in a division some predicted before the season might be the most hotly contested in the NFL.

Player Of The Game

Russell Wilson was 14 for 21 passing for 202 yards and tied a career high with four touchdown passes, all in less than three quarters.

Sidney Rice caught one of Russell Wilson's four touchdown passes late in the first half to help stake the Seahawks to a 24-0 halftime advantage.

By Dean Rutz / The Seattle Times

Game statistics

Jacksonville	0	0	10	7 —	17
Seattle	7	17	14	7 —	45

FIRST QUARTER

Sea—Miller 1 pass from Wilson (Hauschka kick), 8:04. Drive: 7 plays, 71 yards, 3:27.

SECOND QUARTER

Sea—Miller 4 pass from Wilson (Hauschka kick), 14:26. Drive: 6 plays, 40 yards, 2:56.

Sea—Hauschka 21 FG, 9:40. Drive: 5 plays, 44 yards, 2:43.

Sea—Rice 11 pass from Wilson (Hauschka kick), 0:10. Drive: 5 plays, 79 yards, 0:34.

THIRD QUARTER

Jac—Scobee 33 FG, 0:06. Drive: 5 plays, 65 yards, 1:22.

Sea—Rice 23 pass from Wilson (Hauschka kick), 11:41. Drive: 3 plays, 33 yards, 1:26.

Jac—Jones-Drew 2 run (Scobee kick), 6:20. Drive: 2 plays, 2 yards, 0:11.

Sea—Baldwin 35 pass from Jackson (Hauschka kick), 1:28. Drive: 5 plays, 58 yards, 2:26.

FOURTH QUARTER

Jac—Todman 3 run (Scobee kick), 9:06. Drive: 9 plays, 52 yards, 3:09.

Sea—Jackson 5 run (Hauschka kick), 6:32. Drive: 5 plays, 80 yards, 2:34.

Attendance: 68,087.

NET YARDS GAINED

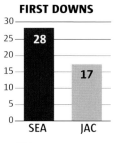

FIRST DOWNS

10	Rushing	6
16	Passing	10
2	Penalties	1

TIME OF POSSESSION

27:25 JAC   32:35 SEA

"An exciting day for the NFC West," said Seattle coach Pete Carroll. "Big day for us, the other teams struggled and all that. Glad we could take advantage of the opportunity to get this win."

And they did so with little real drama.

Seattle entered the game as the largest favorite in franchise history, as much as 20 points depending on the line, and played the role well from the start.

The defense held the Jaguars to three-and-outs on the first four possessions to set a tone of dominance, while the offense played its most efficient game of the season, scoring on four of its seven first-half drives to turn the game into a rout.

Quarterback Russell Wilson led the way, tying a career high with four touchdown passes, two each to tight end Zach Miller and receiver Sidney Rice. Backup Tarvaris Jackson played much of the second half and threw one touchdown pass and ran for another score as the Seahawks piled up 479 yards while holding the Jags to 265.

"Across the board, we played cleaner and sharper," Carroll said. "The way we wanted to."

Maybe most illustrating that point was Seattle had just four penalties after being called for 19 in the first two games.

"We finally took care of an area that's been a big problem for us," Carroll said.

It added up to Seattle's 10th consecutive victory at home and eighth in a row in the regular season.

After the success of the running game in the 29-3 victory over the 49ers, the Seahawks figured the Jaguars might sell out to stop Marshawn Lynch.

"You could see them trying to focus on stopping him in the run game," Miller said.

So the Seahawks repeatedly turned to play-action passes, where Wilson would fake handoffs to Lynch (or sometimes others) and then drop back or roll out and throw.

The plays were successful time and again, including each of the first two touchdowns to Miller.

On the first, a third-and-goal play from the 1, Miller was yards away from any Jacksonville defender as he caught the ball.

"It worked even better today than it did in practice," Miller said.

The play-action success helped Wilson complete 13 of 17 passes for 179 yards in the first half, including 4 of 4 for 69 yards in a 79-yard drive in the final minute of the first half that put the Seahawks ahead 24-0.

That drive came after Wilson had been hit and fumbled, giving Jacksonville the ball in Seattle territory, a threat that ended when Bobby Wagner made an interception.

Wilson then led another short touchdown drive after Seattle's Brandon Mebane recovered a fumble on the first possession of the third quarter to make it 31-0, and the game essentially was over.

Wilson left shortly after that, having completed 14 of 21 passes for 202 yards with only one real mistake, an interception that led to Jacksonville's first touchdown in the third quarter. The performance came a game after he had hit just 8 of 19

against the 49ers.

"We executed when we needed to, in the red zone (scoring four out of five times)," Wilson said. "That's the way we need to play football. When we do that, we're hard to stop."

It's also hard to argue that assessment as Seattle's 3-0 start matches the best in franchise history — it's happened five other times, most recently in 2006 — and leaves the Seahawks as one of just seven undefeated teams in the NFL.

"This is where we want to be," said center Max Unger. "We don't really go into the season thinking we are going to win them all. That's pretty hard, pretty stressful to think about that. But we are in the position that we wanted to be in at the start of the year."

Center Max Unger shows off the hands that begin nearly every Seahawk play. His right fingers are bare, his left wrapped in the tape he wears during games.

By John Lok / The Seattle Times

Hands of the Hawks

A look at Seahawks players' battle-worn paws

By **JAYSON JENKS** | *Seattle Times staff reporter*

Max Unger keeps his right hand at his side. He's hesitant to shake with it.

"My hands are all sweaty," he says.

That's OK, Max. We want your hands in their natural state: mauled, cut, nicked, bruised, busted and, yes, sweaty.

That's what this is about. We wanted to showcase some of the hands that defined the Seahawks' season, from punter Jon Ryan (whose hands are more important than you think) to receiver Sidney Rice (who still carries scars from Brett Favre).

Those are Unger's big paws in the photo above. No hands touch the ball during a game as much as his.

Notice his right hand, the one that snaps the ball

Richard Sherman's hands intercepted eight passes in 2013 to lead the NFL. "Just put them on, create contact," Sherman said. "Disrupt in any way you can."

By John Lok / The Seattle Times

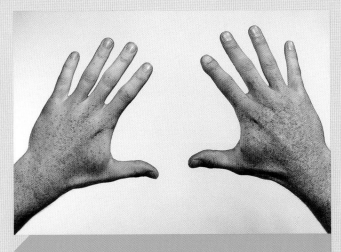

60-some times a game — no glove. He wore one in college but ditched it in the pros. He wants to really feel the ball in his bare hand. Now he just wraps white tape around each finger.

"It's just a little something there," he says, "so if you blow a finger out or something it will stop it a little."

No big deal. They're just hands.

Jon Ryan gets right to the point.

"The biggest thing the average fan might not realize," he says, "is that punting is 80 percent in your hands."

Wait, what?

"The biggest, most important part of punting is your drop," he explains. "Without a good drop, you're giving yourself no shot to hit a good ball."

Ryan, Seattle's veteran punter, is also Seattle's holder for field goals and extra points. He was once selected as an alternate to the Pro Bowl and signed a six-year contract in 2010. The guy has been punting since he was 7 years old; he knows a thing or two about kicking a ball.

"You see so many young guys with these great big legs that can swing hard," he says, "but if they don't have good hands, they're just not going to be a good punter."

Here's the sequence: Catch the ball 14½ yards deep, point the ball slightly nose-down or flat and spin it in your hands so it drops laces-up. Put your elbow against your hip, and there's the line on which Ryan is

trying to drop the ball. And if it's a really windy day, "you're going to drop the ball lower with the nose more down to drive the ball," he says.

From the instant the ball touches his fingertips to when it hits his foot, he has 1.3 seconds.

Sidney Rice smiles and holds his left hand flat. He straightens out his tentacle-like fingers, except one.

His pinkie.

"It won't straighten out," he says.

Sure enough, his little pinkie remains curled like a banana. That would be the result of a game in college, when Rice didn't follow one of the tenets of receiving: see the front of the ball, catch the back.

"I saw the tip," he says, "but I didn't catch the back."

Instead, the ball smashed into the tip of his pinkie and broke the finger at the joint. There's also the time he broke a bone in his right hand while dunking a basketball. He holds out both hands and looks down at the swollen knuckles on his middle fingers.

"And then a little Brett Favre action," he says. "Jammed these up right here."

Rice, Seattle's leading receiver last year, played in Minnesota for two years with the bullet-throwing Favre. Favre throws so hard, Rice says, "The ball catches you, you don't catch it." One time, Favre threw a pass too high for the 6-foot-4 Rice. When Rice turned around in Minnesota's indoor facility, the ball had gone through the insulation in the wall.

Cornerback Richard Sherman doesn't do anything too complicated with his hands.

"Just put them on, create contact," he says. "Disrupt in any way you can. That's the majority of what we're trying to do. We're trying to stop them if we can."

Part of what makes him so effective is his ability to jam receivers at the line, and his hands act as roadblocks.

Watch the way he throws them on a receiver's body, veering him off course and messing with the timing of the play. He's even referred to what he does at the line as "bullying."

Sherman's hands hauled in eight interceptions in 2013, the most in the NFL. He has also twirled his hands in circles around his ears during games, letting opposing players and coaches know they're loco for throwing his way.

See, hands can be practical and playful. That's part of their beauty, no matter how scraped and twisted they may be.

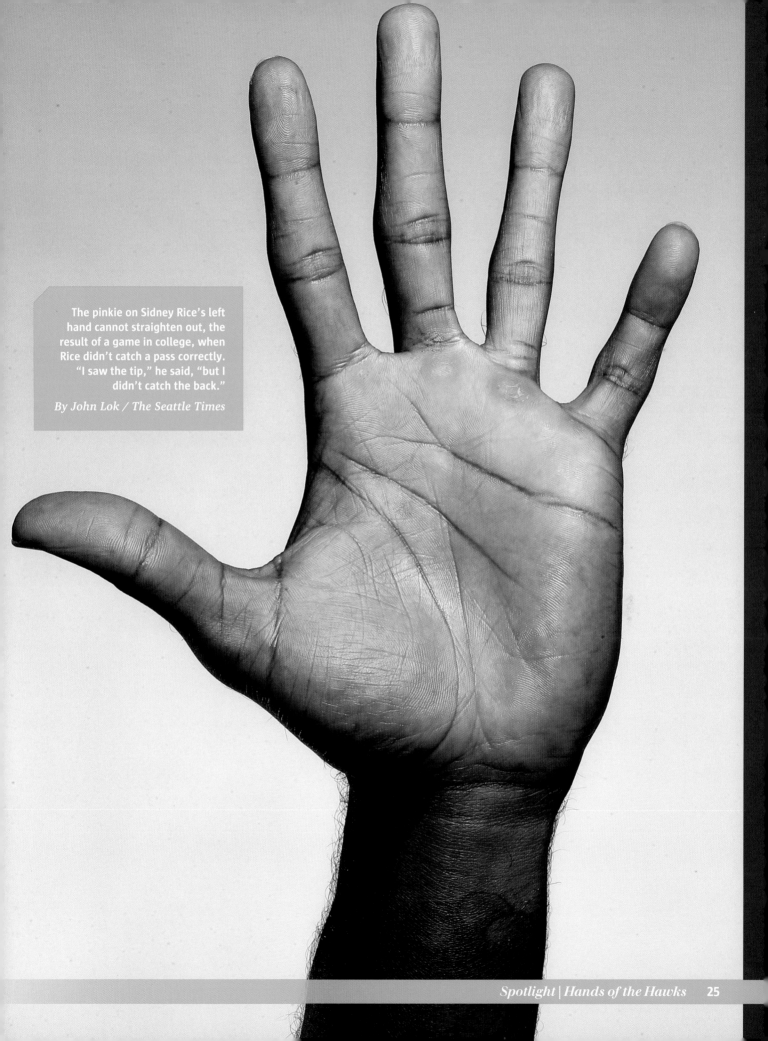

The pinkie on Sidney Rice's left hand cannot straighten out, the result of a game in college, when Rice didn't catch a pass correctly. "I saw the tip," he said, "but I didn't catch the back."

By John Lok / The Seattle Times

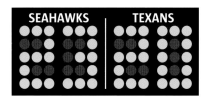

SEAHAWKS   TEXANS

REGULAR SEASON
> GAME 4
Sept. 29, 2013
SEAHAWKS @
TEXANS

FOUR AND OH!

Dramatic comeback in Houston gives Seahawks first-ever 4-0 start

By **BOB CONDOTTA** | *Seattle Times staff reporter*

The Seahawks were battered on defense in the first half in Houston, bruised on offense and soundly beaten in every statistical category.

What hadn't been broken, though, was their confidence — their belief in themselves and each other.

"The mood in the locker room was unbelievable at halftime," quarterback Russell Wilson insisted after the game. "We knew that if we could just hang in there, if we could just play one play at a time, stay in the moment ... and we did that, throughout the whole entire second half."

The Seahawks turned what was an afternoon of misery for most of three quarters into a day of history, rallying from 17 points down to beat the Houston Texans 23-20 in overtime.

The comeback from a 20-3 halftime deficit was the largest for the Seahawks since 1997, and the win improved Seattle's record to 4-0 for the first time since the franchise began play in 1976.

"This is an extraordinary day," said coach Pete Carroll. "That game was all about grit. You just had

Player Of The Game

Quarterback Russell Wilson was not impressive statistically (12 for 23, 123 yards passing, 1 interception) but he made some key plays with his legs (77 yards rushing) and directed a 98-yard drive to get the Seahawks back in the game.

Texans quarterback Matt Schaub was under heavy duress as the Seahawks' Chris Clemons, top , and Clinton McDonald, bottom, bring him down.
By John Lok / The Seattle Times

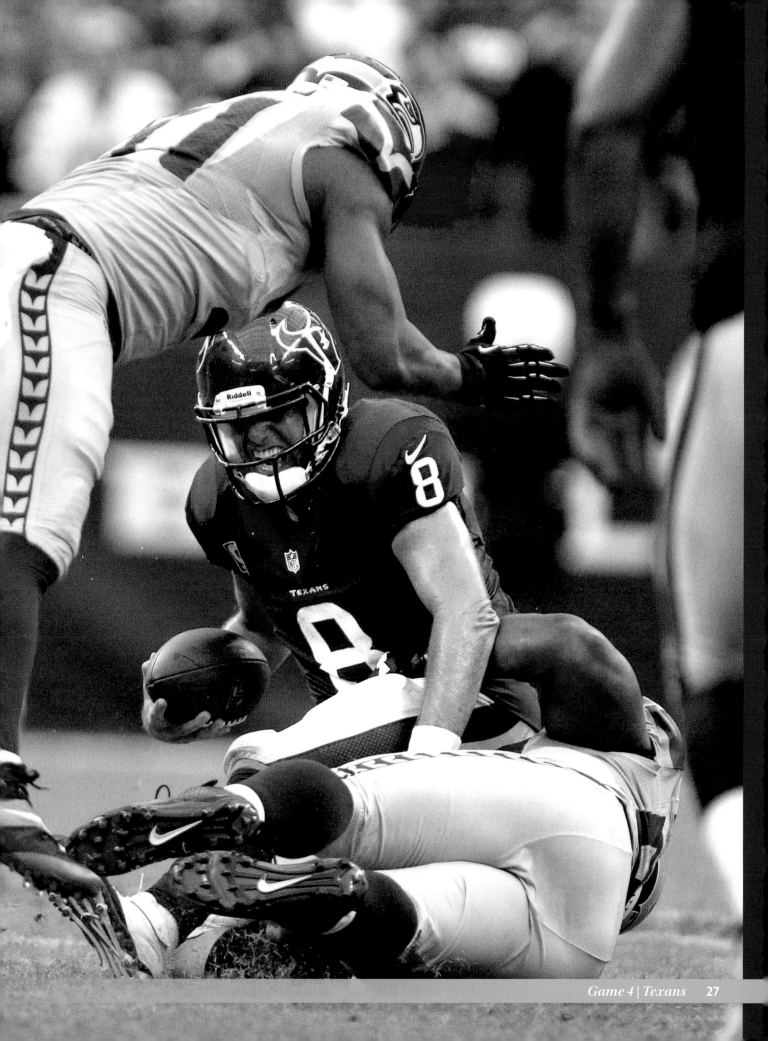

to keep hanging and just not let all the things that had happened build up and stop you from believing."

Steven Hauschka completed the comeback, hitting a 45-yard field goal with 3:19 left in overtime. He was just one of many heroes, though.

There was Richard Sherman picking off an ill-advised pass from Houston's Matt Schaub and returning it 58 yards for a game-tying touchdown with 2:40 remaining in the fourth quarter.

There was Doug Baldwin making a tiptoe catch on the sideline in the fourth quarter to spark Seattle's first significant drive of the game, which cut the Houston lead to a touchdown with 7:43 left in regulation.

And there was Wilson, at times seeming to single-handedly will the Seahawks back after unleashing the reins on his legs in the second half, running for 74 yards after the break.

"We found a way to make some big-time plays in big situations," Wilson said.

In the first half, though, it was all Houston, as the Texans dominated on both sides.

The Texans pushed around a Seattle offensive line playing without three starters, holding the Seahawks to 88 yards and four first downs in the

Game statistics

Seattle	3	0	3	14	3	— 23
Houston	0	20	0	0	0	— 20

FIRST QUARTER

Sea—Hauschka 48 FG, 11:11.
Drive: 4 plays, 40 yards, 1:34.

SECOND QUARTER

Hou—Graham 31 pass from
Schaub (Bullock kick), 14:55.
Drive: 6 plays, 90 yards, 2:52.

Hou—Foster 5 pass from
Schaub (Bullock kick), 6:11.
Drive: 10 plays, 80 yards, 5:10.

Hou—Bullock 22 FG, 3:51.
Drive: 7 plays, 15 yards, 2:13.

Hou—Bullock 42 FG, 0:01.
Drive: 12 plays, 67 yards, 1:12.

THIRD QUARTER

Sea—Hauschka 39 FG, 3:54.
Drive: 4 plays, 0 yards, 0:25.

FOURTH QUARTER

Sea—Lynch 3 run (Hauschka
kick), 7:43. Drive: 14 plays, 98
yards, 7:28.

Sea—Sherman 58 interception
return (Hauschka kick), 2:40.

OVERTIME

Sea—Hauschka 45 FG, 3:19.
Drive: 8 plays, 42 yards, 3:27.

Attendance: 71,756.

NET YARDS GAINED

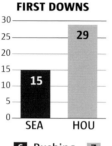

SEA HOU *Passing yards*   SEA HOU *Rushing yards*

FIRST DOWNS

SEA **15**   HOU **29**

6	Rushing	7
6	Passing	20
3	Penalties	2

TIME OF POSSESSION

39:53 HOU   31:48 SEA

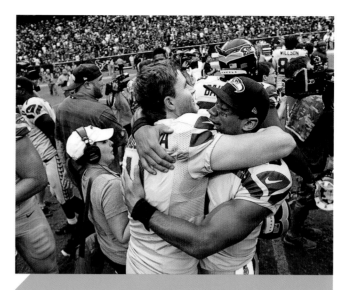

Steven Hauschka, left, and Russell Wilson celebrate after Hauschka's 45-yard field goal in overtime lifted the Seahawks to 4-0 for the first time in franchise history.

By John Lok / The Seattle Times

first half while sacking Wilson twice.

Even more surprising, the Texans plowed through Seattle's defense, which came into the game ranked No. 1 in the NFL, allowing an average of just 241.7 yards in the first three games.

Houston had 324 yards in the first half as Schaub, who rarely was pressured, hit on 17 of 27 passes for 226 yards and two touchdowns.

The only mystery at the half was why the Texans weren't up by more. An Earl Thomas interception, though, stopped one drive inside the 20, and the defense also rose to hold Houston to a field goal after a Marshawn Lynch fumble at Seattle's 19.

Seattle's defenders blamed themselves, many echoing Thomas' comment that "we were just trying to do too much. We were just playing outside ourselves. We got back in at halftime and calmed down."

They also reminded each other that they had been in similar situations before, down 20-0 at half-time against Atlanta in the 2012 postseason before rallying to nearly pull out an improbable win, and

also behind 14-0 against the Redskins before coming back to win.

Still, the result seemed a foregone conclusion when Seattle took over at its own 2, down 20-6, with 11 seconds left in the third quarter. But the Wilson-to-Baldwin pass for 24 yards on third-and-seven — which was ruled a completion after a replay review — got the Seahawks going, and Wilson ran for 4 yards on fourth-and-three later in the drive to lead to a 3-yard Lynch touchdown.

The game again seemed out of reach after Wilson threw a pick with 5:13 left, giving Houston the ball at its own 43 with a 20-13 lead.

On third-and-three from the Seattle 40, though, Schaub got heavy pressure from Kam Chancellor and threw a floating pass that Sherman stepped in front of, and then took to the end zone, losing his shoe in the process. That tied the game at 20 with 2:40 left in regulation.

Seattle — which held the Texans to 152 yards after halftime — then stopped another Houston drive, and two more in overtime, before moving into position for Hauschka's winning kick.

"The character of this team was really challenged today," Carroll said. "There were so many times where we could have said, 'OK, not today.' And they just would not go there."

It was a frustrating day for coach Pete Carroll, left, wide receiver Sidney Rice, bottom, and the Seahawks, who suffered their first loss of the season against the Colts in Indianapolis.

By John Lok / The Seattle Times

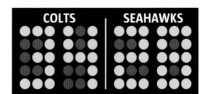

COLTS	SEAHAWKS

REGULAR SEASON
> GAME 5

Oct. 6, 2013
SEAHAWKS @
COLTS

BURNOUT IN INDY

Seahawks suffer first loss despite fast start

By **BOB CONDOTTA** | *Seattle Times staff reporter*

Their first regular-season loss in more than 10 months, the Seattle Seahawks promised afterward, won't linger.

"We'll flush it right after we watch it tomorrow," said Seattle cornerback Richard Sherman after the Colts rallied to beat the Seahawks, 34-28.

Until then, though, they will undoubtedly lament all the missed opportunities and blown chances that led to their nine-game regular-season winning streak coming to an end in Indianapolis.

"We had a lot of situations today that we could have controlled a little bit better, and for whatever reason we didn't make those," said quarterback Russell Wilson after Seattle's first regular-season loss since dropping a 24-21 game at Miami on Nov. 25, 2012.

The Seahawks converted just 2 of 12 third downs on offense, which also forced them to settle for field-goal tries on five of their seven possessions that reached at least the Indianapolis 30.

They allowed the Colts to convert 7 of 12 third downs, including 5 of 6 in the second half as Indianapolis rallied from a 25-17 deficit midway through the third quarter.

The Seahawks allowed a blocked field goal that

Player Of The Game

Jermaine Kearse had only four catches through the first five games, but two of them were for touchdowns. Against the Colts, he caught a 28-yard pass from Russell Wilson late in the first half to help put Seattle in front, 19-14. He also blocked a punt in the first quarter that resulted in a safety.

was returned for a touchdown, turning the momentum of the game after Seattle had for the first time this year gotten off to a fast start, holding a 12-0 lead with just under five minutes left in the first quarter.

And they were penalized seven times for 85 yards, twice on third-down pass-interference calls that kept Colts scoring drives alive.

"The tale of this game will come down to the big plays that they made and they came through on," said Seahawks coach Pete Carroll. "We had our shots and we didn't hit the ones we needed."

For the first 10 minutes or so, though, it looked like Seattle might get a surprisingly easy win in a game that pitted two of the best defenses and rushing attacks in the NFL.

Seattle scored the first two times it had the ball to take a 10-0 lead, then got a blocked punt from Jermaine Kearse that appeared for a moment as it if might be an early back-breaker. But the officials ruled that Jeron Johnson did not control the loose ball in the end zone when he tried to recover it, and Seattle was awarded only a safety and a 12-0 lead.

Then, after stopping Seattle, the Colts took advantage of blown coverage in the Seahawks secondary with a 73-yard Andrew Luck touchdown pass to T.Y. Hilton to get right back in the game.

On Seattle's next possession, a 48-yard field goal attempt by Steven Hauschka was blocked and returned

Game statistics

Seattle ....12 7 9 0 — 28
Indianapolis ..7 10 6 11 — 34

FIRST QUARTER

Sea—Hauschka 42 FG, 11:40. Drive: 5 plays, 28 yards, 2:13.

Sea—Tate 10 pass from Wilson (Hauschka kick), 6:14. Drive: 8 plays, 64 yards, 4:14.

Sea—Punt blocked in end zone for a Safety, 4:53.

Ind—Hilton 73 pass from Luck (Vinatieri kick), 1:04. Drive: 4 plays, 84 yards, 1:41.

SECOND QUARTER

Ind—Howell 61 return of blocked field goal (Vinatieri kick), 13:06.

Sea—Kearse 28 pass from Wilson (Hauschka kick), 5:57. Drive: 12 plays, 82 yards, 7:09.

Ind—Vinatieri 41 FG, 0:58. Drive: 11 plays, 58 yards, 4:59.

THIRD QUARTER

Sea—Hauschka 36 FG, 11:18. Drive: 9 plays, 62 yards, 3:42.

Sea—Hauschka 41 FG, 8:12. Drive: 4 plays, 7 yards, 1:30.

Ind—Hilton 29 pass from Luck (pass failed), 4:16. Drive: 10 plays, 80 yards, 3:56.

Sea—Hauschka 46 FG, 0:35. Drive: 9 plays, 52 yards, 3:41.

FOURTH QUARTER

Ind—Brown 3 run (Luck-Wayne pass), 8:55. Drive: 14 plays, 86 yards, 6:40.

Ind—Vinatieri 49 FG, 1:55. Drive: 9 plays, 42 yards, 4:43.

Attendance: 66,608.

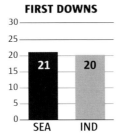

NET YARDS GAINED

SEA IND — *Passing yards*
SEA IND — *Rushing yards*

FIRST DOWNS

SEA	IND
21	20

11 Rushing 6
10 Passing 12
0 Penalties 2

TIME OF POSSESSION

28:38 IND 31:22 SEA

Jeron Johnson tried to score a touchdown off a blocked punt but the Seahawks were instead awarded a safety that staked them to a 12-0 lead in the first quarter.

By John Lok / The Seattle Times

---

61 yards for a touchdown by Delano Howell, turning what could have been a two-possession Seattle lead into a sudden two-point deficit.

Although the Seahawks got the lead back and held it much of the rest of the way, they never again seemed to have control.

A Wilson touchdown pass of 28 yards to Kearse gave Seattle a 19-17 halftime lead.

But in the second half, all Seattle could manage was three Hauschka field goals on three possessions inside the Colts' 29.

"We really struggled on third down," Carroll said. "All those turning into field goals ... that would have made a huge difference."

Still, Seattle held a 28-23 lead going into the fourth quarter, and was generally moving the ball well — the Seahawks finished with 423 yards, with Wilson and Marshawn Lynch each rushing for 102 yards.

Seattle looked like it had the Colts stopped on their initial fourth-quarter possession when a third-down pass to Hilton fell incomplete. But a flag fell, officials calling Sherman for interference.

"That's how it is on the road," Sherman said with a smile that suggested he wanted to say more.

Luck then converted two more third-down throws, the second one after the Colts challenged a spot that had them coming up just short and got the call reversed.

Two plays later, Donald Brown scored on a 3-yard run, and a two-point conversion made it 31-28 with 8:55 left.

Seattle, which punted only twice, then went three-and-out. The Colts responded with a 42-yard drive that consumed 4:33 and concluded with another Adam Vinatieri field goal to make it 34-28 with 1:55 left.

Seattle had twice earlier in the season rallied in the fourth quarter on the road — at Carolina and at Houston.

And this drive started promisingly with a 22-yard Wilson run. But then came two incomplete passes, a delay-of-game penalty, another incomplete pass, and finally a Wilson pass thrown under heavy pressure that was picked off by Darius Butler, essentially ending the game with 1:23 left.

"I love those situations," Wilson said. "To have the ball, 1:55 left — that's all I can ask for. Normally we make that, and for whatever reason, we didn't today."

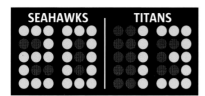

SEAHAWKS **TITANS**

REGULAR SEASON
> GAME 6

Oct. 13, 2013
SEAHAWKS @
TITANS

RUGGED REBOUND

Seahawks bounce back with less-than-perfect win over Titans

By BOB CONDOTTA | *Seattle Times staff reporter*

For a split second, Russell Wilson morphed from quarterback to safety.

It was four plays into the fourth quarter, and Tennessee's Zach Brown had his eyes on a bouncing ball that had just been blasted away from Marshawn Lynch, a go-ahead touchdown in his sights.

Brown, though, couldn't quite get a handle on the ball, forced to watch in frustration as Wilson — who had been preparing to make a tackle — corralled it instead.

"I felt like I was playing shortstop again," said Wilson, who played one year of minor-league baseball. "I got the big hop and went and got it. That's what they teach you in baseball."

Three plays later, it was the Seahawks who instead took the lead for good en route to a 20-13 win over the Tennessee Titans in front of 68,127 at CenturyLink Field.

And it only made sense that it was Wilson who proved a rare player able to control the football on a day when it often seemed to have a mind of its own.

Seattle, 5-1 and still atop the NFC West, had five fumbles, losing two (including one that turned

Richard Sherman celebrates with Kam Chancellor after making an interception early in the fourth quarter. On the Seahawks' ensuing possession, Marshawn Lynch scored on a 3-yard touchdown to put the game out of reach.

By John Lok / The Seattle Times

Player Of The Game

Running back Marshawn Lynch finished with 155 total yards, including 78 yards on four receptions. He also rushed 21 times for 77 yards and two touchdowns.

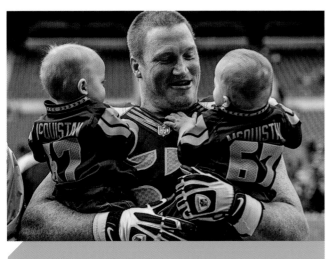

Paul McQuistan enjoys a moment with two of his biggest fans, his 9-month-old twins Shane and Shawn.

By Dean Rutz / The Seattle Times

Game statistics

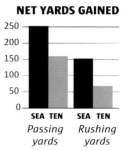

Tennessee	3	7	0	3 —	13
Seattle	0	7	3	10 —	20

FIRST QUARTER
Ten—Bironas 38 FG, 5:16.
Drive: 9 plays, 72 yards, 4:43.

SECOND QUARTER
Sea—Lynch 1 run (Hauschka kick), 2:41. Drive: 12 plays, 74 yards, 6:42.
Ten—McCourty 77 fumble return (Bironas kick), 0:00.

THIRD QUARTER
Sea—Hauschka 31 FG, 4:27.
Drive: 12 plays, 75 yards, 6:26.

FOURTH QUARTER
Sea—Hauschka 29 FG, 11:23.
Drive: 7 plays, 69 yards, 3:37.
Sea—Lynch 3 run (Hauschka kick), 7:33. Drive: 7 plays, 59 yards, 3:42.
Ten—Bironas 25 FG, 2:18.
Drive: 14 plays, 69 yards, 5:15.
Attendance: 68,127.

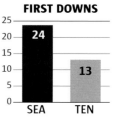

NET YARDS GAINED

FIRST DOWNS

	SEA	TEN
Rushing	11	3
Passing	10	8
Penalties	3	2

TIME OF POSSESSION

26:38 TEN   33:22 SEA

into Tennessee's only touchdown of the game), while the Titans also had three (losing none) along with throwing two interceptions.

"We had some fluke plays out there today," Wilson said.

Flukiest was a 77-yard fumble return by Tennessee's Jason McCourty when Seattle backup holder Chris Maragos had the ball ripped from him after he fumbled a snap on a field-goal attempt. Maragos was holding because punter Jon Ryan — the usual holder — was kicking, filling in because Steven Hauschka had been injured while trying to make a tackle on a kickoff.

"We made enough mistakes to make it a close game," said Seattle coach Pete Carroll.

It was Wilson who provided the stability, along with a return-to-form game from the Seattle defense, that allowed the Seahawks to pull away.

Wilson was 23 for 31 for 257 yards and no interceptions, including 4 for 4 for 100 yards on two fourth-quarter scoring drives that gave the Seahawks the lead for good.

Wilson also ran 10 times for 61 yards and expertly executed a hard count to draw Tennessee offsides on third-and-four on the final drive of the game, bringing a merciful end.

"I felt like I was really in tune with the game," Wilson said. "And that's where I want to be every week."

Also back in the proper key was a defense that a week ago allowed 34 points (27 coming directly against the defense) in a loss to the Colts.

The Titans had just two drives longer than 31 yards, only once getting closer than the Seattle 21-yard line.

After a 29-yard Hauschka field goal, which followed Wilson's save of Lynch's fumble, put Seattle ahead 13-10 with 11:23 left in the game, the defense made the play that turned the tide for good.

To no surprise, it was Richard Sherman who made it, picking off a deep pass from Ryan Fitzpatrick intended for Nate Washington. Seattle took the ball at the Tennessee 41, and Wilson quickly completed three passes before a Lynch 3-yard touchdown run with 7:33 remaining finally gave Seattle some breathing room.

Sherman had been beaten for a key touchdown in the loss to the Colts, but had vowed it wouldn't happen again.

"We were frustrated with our performance last week because we easily could have played way more sound and eliminated those big plays," he said.

The Titans' Darius Reynaud delivered a crushing blow to the unlikeliest would-be tackler on the Seahawks: kicker Steven Hauschka, who left the game briefly.

By John Lok / The Seattle Times

It was that sense of control that allowed the Seahawks to feel as if they were still in control, even when the Titans took a 10-7 lead at halftime after the McCourty fumble return.

Seattle had been held to just two first downs on its first three drives, but the offense got going in the second quarter. A 74-yard drive led to a Lynch 1-yard touchdown run to put Seattle ahead, and the Seahawks seemed ready to tack on more before the ill-fated field-goal attempt.

Seattle kicked with the ball at the Tennessee 4 and two seconds left. Carroll said later that he should have gone for it instead of putting the backup battery into the game.

"I screwed it up," he said.

Players said not to worry.

"They hadn't scored on our defense and we were feeling good about our offense," Sherman said of the mood at halftime.

When the gun sounded, Wilson was able to walk off CenturyLink Field in the same fashion as he has every other game he has played there — in victory — Seattle having won 11 straight home games, all occurring since Wilson took over at quarterback.

Rare glimpse at soft side of Beast Mode

Tough runner describes Beast Quake run as a metaphor for his life

By LARRY STONE | *Seattle Times columnist*

When it comes to Marshawn Lynch's mindset — a hot Seahawks topic — we're pretty much left to interpreting his gestures, parsing his body language, reading between the lines.

These days, of course, there is much to ask the enigmatic running back. It would be great to probe Lynch's thoughts about how his season evolved, his role in the offense, and his reaction to not getting the ball at the goal line in back-to-back weeks.

Instead, Lynch has chosen, for the most part, to remain silent with the media. That is his prerogative. But after watching the extended interview Lynch did with ESPN's Jeffrey Chadiha for an "E:60" segment, I can't help but lament what we're missing.

In the piece, which focused on how Lynch's rough Oakland, Calif., upbringing has shaped his personality, the 27-year-old came across as sincere and compassionate.

His analysis of the 2011 Beast Quake run, in which Lynch portrayed that signature play in the postseason as an extended metaphor for his life, was one of the most profound answers I've ever heard from any athlete:

"Growing up, being where I'm from, a lot of people don't see the light. I didn't see the light in that play. Went forward, ran into some trouble. Being on food stamps, living in the projects. Running head-first into linebackers. Start to play football. Things opened up for me a little bit. Breaking a couple more tackles.

"He's a very unique individual, and he is himself 100 percent of the time," Richard Sherman said of Marshawn Lynch, here celebrating a touchdown with teammates during the game against the Vikings.

By Bettina Hansen / The Seattle Times

Going to jail. Getting in trouble. Coming out of that. Touchdown.

"I guess you could say that run is symbolic of my life."

Lynch didn't shy away from the stumbles that have plagued him since he turned pro in 2007 — a gun charge, a hit-and-run incident, a DUI.

When asked about the perception that he is a thug, Lynch became emotional, tearing up before answering.

"I would like to see them (critics) grow up in project housing authorities, being racially profiled growing up, sometimes not even having nothing to eat, sometimes having to wear the same damn clothes to school for a whole week. Then all of a sudden a big-ass change in their life, like their dream come true, to the point they're starting their career, at 20 years old, when they still don't know (bleep). I would like to see some of the mistakes they would make."

Clearly, there is a deep reservoir of emotions churning within Lynch.

But with rare exceptions — and never more openly than with Chadiha — Lynch has chosen to share his innermost feelings only with teammates, friends and family.

Just about the only other public access to Lynch these days comes via his ubiquitous plumbing commercial, which shows a playful side that teammates say is part of his persona.

"He's got a sense of humor to him," said fellow running back Robert Turbin. "I'm glad he did those things so people can see he's not what they perceive, this macho dude. He's just regular. He's cool."

Richard Sherman calls Lynch "one of the most misunderstood people in the game. I think he's a great philanthropist. He does anything for kids. He'll tell you

Lynch by the numbers

Lynch rushed for 1,257 yards in 2013, the third straight season he surpassed 1,200 yards. He also set a career high for receiving yards with 316.

Game 1 at Panthers
17 rushes, **43 yards**, 0 TDs

Game 2 vs. 49ers
28 rushes, **98 yards**, 2 TDs

Game 3 vs. Jaguars
17 rushes, **69 yards**, 0 TDs

Game 4 at Texans
17 rushes, **98 yards**, 1 TD

Game 5 at Colts
17 rushes, **102 yards**, 0 TDs

Game 6 vs. Titans
21 rushes, **77 yards**, 2 TDs

Game 7 at Cardinals
21 rushes, **91 yards**, 1 TD

Game 8 at Rams
8 rushes, **23 yards**, 0 TDs

Game 9 vs. Bucs
21 rushes, **125 yards**, 0 TDs

Game 10 at Falcons
24 rushes, **145 yards**, 1 TD

Game 11 vs. Vikings
17 rushes, **54 yards**, 2 TDs

Game 12 vs. Saints
16 rushes, **45 yards**, 0 TDs

Game 13 at 49ers
20 rushes, **72 yards**, 1 TD

Game 14 at Giants
16 rushes, **47 yards**, 1 TD

Game 15 vs. Cardinals
18 rushes, **71 yards**, 0 TDs

Game 16 vs. Rams
23 rushes, **97 yards**, 1 TD

that before anything. If there's adults around, he'll just be like, 'Whatever. Basically you guys get out the way.'

"But if there's a bunch of kids, he'll do whatever he can to help them, to make sure that they have everything they need, to make sure that they get a better chance, and he does it in his own unique way. And I think that if more people saw that side of him, they would look at him differently."

So I asked Sherman if he would like to see Lynch show that side more frequently. His answer cuts to the paradox that is Beast Mode.

"I wouldn't, to tell you the truth, because that's not him. There's one thing about Marshawn, he's himself, all the time. He doesn't sugar coat anything. He doesn't try to disguise and be someone else. He's a very unique individual, and he is himself 100 percent of the time. I respect the world out of him for being himself all the time because he's genuine."

The conclusion is, Lynch is deeper than we think, but part of his mystique is the mystery.

As Michael Robinson correctly noted, much of the power of the "E:60" segment came from Lynch's reticence. So rare are his public pronouncements that when he opens himself up like that, it's riveting.

Robinson, who is close to Lynch, agrees there is much more to the running back than meets the eye.

"He cares a lot more about his teammates than people think. He cares a lot more about this game than people think. He wants to be great a lot more than what people think. He wants to be the best a lot more than what people think. He's just not a guy that's going to do it for the camera. That's how he is."

And that, apparently, is how he'll stay.

Marchawn Lynch provided a rare glimpse into who he is in a TV segment broadcast during the 2013 season. Of his Beast Quake run, he told ESPN, "I guess you could say that run is symbolic of my life."

By John Lok / The Seattle Times

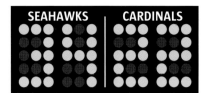

SEAHAWKS | CARDINALS

REGULAR SEASON
> GAME 7

Oct. 17, 2013
SEAHAWKS @
CARDINALS

EARLY BIRDS

Fast beginning propels Seahawks to their first-ever 6-1 start

By BOB CONDOTTA | *Seattle Times staff reporter*

While the Seahawks teetered briefly after again taking a big, early lead on the road, there was no collapse this time.

And that ability to stand tall in the face of adversity spoke as loudly to coach Pete Carroll as anything else that emerged from a 34-22 win over the Arizona Cardinals in Glendale, Ariz.

"For a young bunch of guys, we have a very strong resolve about the ups and downs and the rigors of it," Carroll said after Seattle improved to 6-1 for the first time in its history. "It's just kind of characteristic of the way we deal with stuff. We don't like it when things aren't going right, but it isn't going to faze us. We aren't going to lose our cool."

The Seahawks had their chance to after taking a 14-0 lead and then seeing it largely dissolve due mostly to their errors.

Arizona twice got within four points, which brought back eerie memories of the loss at Indianapolis when Seattle led 12-0 early only to lose 34-28.

This time, though, the Seahawks responded swiftly and strongly to easily put away the Cardinals in a building where they had lost six of their last seven games.

Player Of The Game

Running back Marshawn Lynch had another effective game, rushing for 91 yards on 21 carries and playing a key role in Seattle's two touchdown drives in the third quarter. His 2-yard scoring run late in the third quarter made it 31-13 and put the game away.

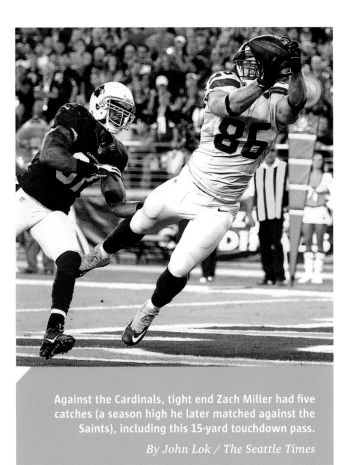

Against the Cardinals, tight end Zach Miller had five catches (a season high he later matched against the Saints), including this 15-yard touchdown pass.

By John Lok / The Seattle Times

Game statistics

Seattle	7	10	14	3	— 34
Arizona	0	10	3	9	— 22

FIRST QUARTER

Sea — Rice 31 pass from Wilson (Hauschka kick), 7:13. Drive: 5 plays, 83 yards, 2:31.

SECOND QUARTER

Sea — Miller 15 pass from Wilson (Hauschka kick), 13:25. Drive: 11 plays, 72 yards, 5:26.

Ari — Feely 49 FG, 4:02. Drive: 11 plays, 26 yards, 6:10.

Ari — Mendenhall 3 run (Feely kick), 3:40. Drive: 1 plays, 3 yards, 0:03.

Sea — Hauschka 51 FG, 0:05. Drive: 12 plays, 47 yards, 3:35.

THIRD QUARTER

Ari — Feely 52 FG, 11:48. Drive: 5 plays, 17 yards, 1:09.

Sea — Davis 1 pass from Wilson (Hauschka kick), 7:48. Drive: 10 plays, 80 yards, 4:00.

Sea — Lynch 2 run (Hauschka kick), 3:52. Drive: 2 plays, 1 yards, 0:51.

FOURTH QUARTER

Ari — Feely 22 FG, 14:41. Drive: 6 plays, 11 yards, 0:39.

Sea — Hauschka 42 FG, 10:21. Drive: 8 plays, 56 yards, 4:20.

Ari — Brown 8 pass from Palmer (pass failed), 4:34. Drive: 8 plays, 71 yards, 3:28.

Attendance: 61,200.

NET YARDS GAINED

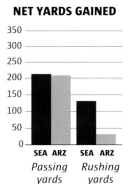

SEA ARZ	SEA ARZ
Passing yards	*Rushing yards*

FIRST DOWNS

SEA	ARZ
21	22

6	Rushing	2
14	Passing	16
1	Penalties	4

TIME OF POSSESSION

32:20 ARZ — 27:40 SEA

"The talk on the sidelines was just hang in there," said safety Kam Chancellor. "You know you are going to have adversity in games sometimes, but the stronger team always comes out and wins in the end."

That Seattle was, holding the Cardinals to 234 yards, 30 on the ground, and making a season-high seven sacks.

"Their offensive line, we knew that they had some weak points in there so we took advantage of it," linebacker K.J. Wright said.

Seattle drove smoothly for touchdowns on each of its first two possessions, each of the scores coming on passes by Wilson — the first going 31 yards to Sidney Rice, who had lost a fumble a week ago that Carroll had called unacceptable, and the second a 15-yarder to tight end Zach Miller, out the last two games with a hamstring injury.

Seattle forced another punt on its next drive and for a second appeared to have a 21-0 lead as Golden Tate returned the kick for a touchdown.

However, the play was nullified due to a penalty for blocking in the back on Mike Morgan.

Seattle moved to the Arizona 43, deciding to go for it on fourth-and-one.

That proved ill-fated when Wilson was stopped for no gain on a quarterback sneak.

Arizona drove for a field goal, and then got right back in the game when Wilson fumbled as he was sacked by Matt Shaughnessy, with Calais Campbell recovering at the Seattle 3-yard line, one of three Wilson fumbles (losing two) on the night.

"That's on me," Wilson said. "I'll make sure I get that right."

That led to a 3-yard touchdown run by Rashard Mendenhall that allowed Arizona to be within 17-10 at the half despite Seattle holding a 210-69 edge in yards.

Arizona drove for a field goal on its first
possession of the third quarter, and for one of
the few times the home crowd was louder than a
boisterous group of Seattle fans.

On Seattle's next drive, with the Seahawks
facing a third-and-three from the Arizona 48,
Wilson was able to get off a pass as he was being
tackled by linebacker Daryl Washington — many
in the crowd already cheering the apparent sack
— finding Miller for a 6-yard completion.

"I knew I wasn't down," Wilson said. "I just
made a little shortstop flip to him."

Marshawn Lynch followed a few plays later
with a punishing run up the middle in which he
carried several Cardinal defenders.

Wilson capped the drive with a 1-yard touchdown pass to Kellen Davis to make it 24-13, and
the game was never really again in doubt.

Browner then returned an interception to
the 1, drawing laughs from teammates — and
likely ribbing into next week — by falling down

on his own.

"We're going to be in his head for quite a little
bit," Chancellor said, laughing.

Seattle's defense then spent much of the rest
of the night turning the University of Phoenix
Stadium into its own dance floor.

Defenders took turns showing off their signature moves after sacks, such as Michael Bennett's
belly roll and Malcolm Smith's "Hawk-Eyes."

"It's fun ball," said cornerback Richard Sherman. "It's fun, it's exciting."

It also left Seattle assured of being alone atop
the NFC West and at least tied for the lead in the
NFC at the end of Week 7.

Golden Tate came up with a touchdown on this third-quarter play in which he outmaneuvered Janoris Jenkins and then outran the St. Louis defense. He was later fined by the NFL for taunting while running the final 30 yards.

By John Lok / The Seattle Times

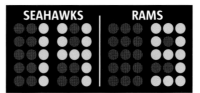

GREAT ESCAPE

Defense makes winning goal-line stand at the end

By BOB CONDOTTA | *Seattle Times staff reporter*

For most of the game, the Seahawks could barely move an inch, let alone a yard.

When it mattered most, though, neither could the St. Louis Rams.

And a valiant goal-line stand by the Seattle defense in St. Louis allowed the Seahawks to escape with a 14-9 victory over the Rams in a "Monday Night Football" game they entered as two-touchdown favorites.

Seattle was outgained 339-135 and allowed as many sacks as it got first downs — seven of each.

Yet when it was over, Seattle had the most important seven of all — its seventh victory of the season, improving to 7-1 for the first time in team history.

"Very fortunate to get out of here (with a win)," said Seattle coach Pete Carroll. "I think everyone who watched that one could see we were very fortunate."

St. Louis took over at its own 3 with 5:42 to play and drove to the Seattle 1-yard line with less than a minute left.

But on third-and-goal from the 1 with 27 sec-

Player Of The Game

Wide receiver Golden Tate had five catches for 93 yards, 80 of those coming on a third-quarter touchdown reception. He also scored Seattle's other touchdown on a 2-yard catch in the second quarter.

The Seahawks stopped the Rams' Daryl Richardson on third-and-goal from the Seattle 1-yard line late in the fourth quarter. The Seahawks completed the goal-line stand by forcing an incomplete pass on fourth down.

By John Lok / The Seattle Times

Game statistics

Seattle ....0 7 7 0 — 14
St. Louis ......3 0 3 3 — 9

FIRST QUARTER
StL—Zuerlein 33 FG, 4:37.
Drive: 7 plays, 31 yards, 3:27.

SECOND QUARTER
Sea—Tate 2 pass from Wilson (Hauschka kick), 5:37. Drive: 6 plays, 26 yards, 2:41.

THIRD QUARTER
StL—Zuerlein 28 FG, 4:01.
Drive: 10 plays, 37 yards, 5:51.

Sea—Tate 80 pass from Wilson (Hauschka kick), 3:45. Drive: 2 plays, 80 yards, 0:16.

FOURTH QUARTER
StL—Zuerlein 27 FG, 12:51.
Drive: 11 plays, 69 yards, 5:54.
Attendance: 55,966.

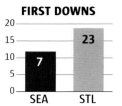

NET YARDS GAINED

FIRST DOWNS

SEA 7
STL 23

	1 Rushing	12
	4 Passing	7
	2 Penalties	4

TIME OF POSSESSION

38:09 STL   21:51 SEA

onds left, backup middle linebacker Heath Farwell — a regular member of Seattle's goal-line unit — led a charge to stop Daryl Richardson for no gain.

Then as time ran out, a corner blitz helped lead to a hurried pass by St. Louis quarterback Kellen Clemens to Brian Quick that fell incomplete under heavy coverage from Seattle cornerback Brandon Browner.

The third-down play might have been even more critical, coming after an offsides penalty on Seattle's Chris Clemens moved St. Louis to a couple feet of the goal line.

Farwell, a special-teams demon who hadn't been on the field for a defensive snap until that point, said he had a good idea what the Rams might do.

"I saw the offensive linemen in a four-point stance so I knew it was going to be a downhill run, they had a near back to me that was coming right at me so I had a feeling," he said. "So I kind of cheated up expecting the power and ran through the gap and was fortunate enough to be able to get a decent hit (on Richardson)."

Safety Earl Thomas said that made the final play easier to defend, saying he knew at that point it would be a pass.

"You expect that because we did a great job stopping the run (on third down)," Thomas said. "Heath did a great job putting his nose in there and getting a hat on the running back and slowing him up."

When it was over, Thomas felt like collapsing, not so much in disbelief but in utter exhaustion.

"I never get tired but today was my most physical game I think I have ever played," he said.

The game felt odd from the start with the Edward Jones Dome maybe half full (despite a listed attendance of 55,966) with Game 5 of the World Series being played a mile away.

St. Louis, though, seemed inspired despite the flood of empty seats, dominating the Seahawks from the beginning.

The Seahawks, however, led 7-3 at halftime thanks to a Richard Sherman interception returned to the Rams' 29-yard-line that led to a 2-yard scoring pass from Russell Wilson to Golden Tate.

The Seahawks were no more offensive in the second half except for one play — an 80-yard

Wilson-to-Tate hookup with 3:45 to play in the third quarter.

Even that score, though, hardly came bathed in glory.

On the play, Tate leapt over cornerback Janoris Jenkins to grab the pass and then had a free path into the end zone. Tate, though, took his time getting there, holding the ball with one hand and waving with the other to taunt Jenkins and safety Rodney McLeod as he ran the final 30 yards or so. That drew a 15-yard personal foul for taunting but didn't negate the touchdown.

"My emotions got the best of me," said Tate, who said that the Seattle receivers and Rams defensive backs had been "chirping" all game.

But while Carroll said it's obvious the Seahawks have a lot of work to do, the Seahawks also noted that they have played five of eight on the road and won four, and remain in first place in the NFC West.

Even if the margin felt as thin as could be.

"If there's a blade of grass to defend we are going to defend it," Farwell said. "We didn't expect them to score. We expected to stop them. It didn't matter if they had 1 yard or 1 inch."

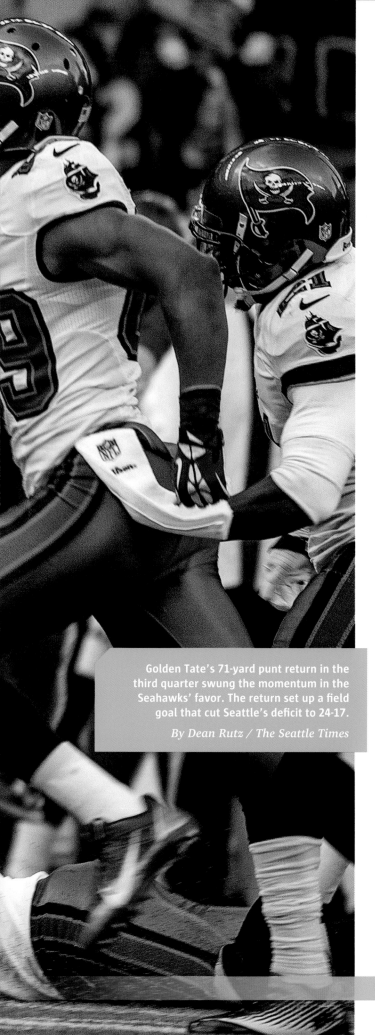

Golden Tate's 71-yard punt return in the third quarter swung the momentum in the Seahawks' favor. The return set up a field goal that cut Seattle's deficit to 24-17.

By Dean Rutz / The Seattle Times

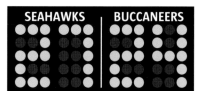

SEAHAWKS | BUCCANEERS

REGULAR SEASON
> GAME 9

Nov. 3, 2013
BUCCANEERS @
SEAHAWKS

DISASTER AVERTED

Seahawks need record rally against Bucs to improve to NFC-best 8-1

By BOB CONDOTTA | *Seattle Times staff reporter*

History may not remember that Golden Tate actually didn't score a touchdown on his 71-yard punt return.

In fact, all the Seahawks got out of it was a field goal.

But after Seattle had rallied to defeat the Tampa Bay Buccaneers 27-24 in overtime, many pointed to Tate's return as the moment the game changed in the Seahawks' favor.

It was the moment it became apparent the Seahawks truly would turn the potential infamy of losing at home as a 16-point favorite — only one time had they ever been favored by more — into the history of rallying from 21 points down, the biggest comeback in Seattle's 38 years as an NFL franchise.

"That just kind of let you know that we're here, that we're coming for this win," said Seattle coach Pete Carroll. "It was an incredible play."

Even if at first, many watching probably were using a different adjective as Tate drifted to his own 4-yard line to catch the ball with just over a minute

Player Of The Game

Running back Marshawn Lynch rushed for a season-high 125 yards on 21 carries and added four receptions for 16 yards. He surpassed his rushing total from the previous game (23 yards) during the first possession (43 yards on four carries) and was the go-to player on the winning drive in overtime.

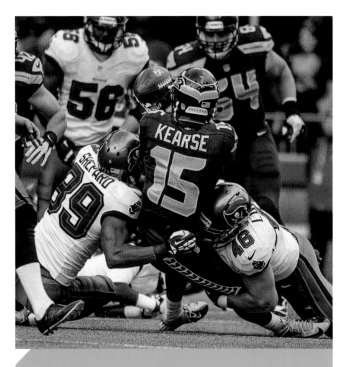

Jermaine Kearse fumbles a kickoff return, which eventually led to a Buccaneers touchdown that put the Seahawks in a 21-0 hole in the second quarter.

By Dean Rutz / The Seattle Times

Game statistics

Tampa Bay 0 21 3 0 0 — 24
Seattle   0 7 7 10 3 — 27

SECOND QUARTER

TB — Wright 12 pass from Glennon (Lindell kick), 11:50. Drive: 10 plays, 90 yards, 6:03.

TB — Underwood 20 pass from Glennon (Lindell kick), 2:55. Drive: 11 plays, 84 yards, 6:42.

TB — Crabtree 2 pass from James (Lindell kick), 2:16. Drive: 2 plays, 31 yards, 0:30.

Sea — Kearse 16 pass from Wilson (Hauschka kick), 1:40. Drive: 3 plays, 80 yards, 0:36.

THIRD QUARTER

TB — Lindell 33 FG, 9:48. Drive: 11 plays, 65 yards, 5:12.

Sea — Wilson 10 run (Hauschka kick), 5:00. Drive: 9 plays, 86 yards, 4:48.

FOURTH QUARTER

Sea — Hauschka 36 FG, 14:47. Drive: 4 plays, 7 yards, 1:11.

Sea — Baldwin 10 pass from Wilson (Hauschka kick), 1:51. Drive: 10 plays, 59 yards, 4:22.

OVERTIME

Sea — Hauschka 27 FG, 8:11. Drive: 9 plays, 51 yards, 4:53.

Attendance: 67,873.

NET YARDS GAINED

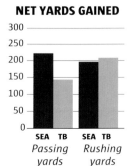

SEA TB   SEA TB
*Passing   Rushing
yards   yards*

FIRST DOWNS

26 24

SEA   TB

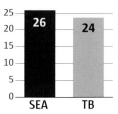

12 Rushing **11**
11 Passing **10**
3 Penalties **3**

TIME OF POSSESSION

36:37 TB   30:12 SEA

left in the third quarter and Seattle trailing 24-14.

"You can't be timid," said quarterback Russell Wilson. "You've got to be able to step up and make a play."

Tate did just that, breaking or evading six tackles as he crisscrossed the field before being tackled at the Tampa Bay 25.

"We were down; we needed something to happen," Tate said. "Once I got the ball in my hands, I just played backyard football."

The Seahawks were forced to settle for a 36-yard Steven Hauschka field goal on the ensuing possession. But that cut the lead to 24-17 and seemed to create a sense of inevitability on each sideline as to how the game would finish.

"You could see the momentum shift, and the crowd got into it and got pumped," said Tampa Bay cornerback Darrelle Revis, who called it "probably the biggest play of the game."

From there, Seattle dominated as Tampa Bay got only two first downs the rest of the game and just 37 yards on four possessions in the fourth quarter and overtime. The Seattle offense, meanwhile,

got a 10-yard pass from Wilson to Doug Baldwin with 1:51 left to force overtime. In overtime, the Seahawks completed the comeback with a 51-yard, Marshawn Lynch-led drive to set up Hauschka's 27-yard game-winning field goal with 8:11 left.

Seattle's previous largest comeback was 20 points in Denver on Dec. 20, 1995. In that game, the Seahawks were down 20-0 before winning 31-27.

It was also the fourth time this year Seattle has won a game in which it was behind or tied going into the fourth quarter — and that doesn't count the previous game's final-play escape at St. Louis.

"The last two weeks we've just been making it harder on ourselves than we need it to be," safety Earl Thomas said. "But we are winning ugly, and that just shows we are never out of the game."

The Seahawks won despite allowing at least 200 yards rushing (205) for the second straight week against a team that previously hadn't been very effective on the ground. They won despite giving up

three turnovers while not getting any, the first time all year they hadn't forced a takeaway. And they won despite allowing three first-half touchdown passes.

Carroll seemed most concerned about the run defense.

"Right now we're in a little bit of a funk (in defending the run)," Carroll said. "We're not tackling very well."

Tampa Bay rookie Mike James, stepping in for an injured Doug Martin, finished with 158 yards, helping set up three second-quarter touchdowns.

Two came in the span of 39 seconds as the Bucs jumped out to a 21-0 lead. Two Mike Glennon touchdown passes (a 12-yarder to Tim Wright and a 20-yarder to Tiquan Underwood) made it 14-0. Then Jermaine Kearse fumbled a kickoff, setting up a James touchdown pass on a trick play from the 2-yard line.

Baldwin said that despite the team's never-say-quit mantras, "we are human. I looked at the score-board and saw it was 21-0 and I was like 'Damn, something's got to change.'"

It did in a hurry as Wilson led a quick touch-down drive, capped by a 16-yard TD pass to Kearse, to make it 21-7 at halftime.

A 10-yard Wilson TD run with five minutes left in the third quarter made it 24-14. On Tampa Bay's next drive, a holding penalty set the Bucs back, leading to the punt that Tate brought back into Tampa Bay territory.

Carroll and Tate said that on other days, in other situations, the prudent course might have been to let the ball roll into the end zone. But that day wasn't Sunday.

"I thought the time was right to make that play and make something happen," Tate said.

Russell Wilson and the Seahawks had to scratch and claw against Lavonte David and the Buccaneers, who entered the game winless. The Seahawks' rally from a 21-point deficit was the greatest in franchise history.

By Bettina Hansen / The Seattle Times

Russell Wilson threw for more yards, more touchdowns and fewer interceptions in his second year than in his rookie year.

By Bettina Hansen / The Seattle Times

Russell Wilson 2.0

The Seahawks quarterback was even better in his second season

By **JAYSON JENKS** | *Seattle Times staff reporter*

The camera cut to Russell Wilson, hoping to capture a juicy reaction. It's one of the most popular tricks in television:

The moment after a good or bad play, cut to a close-up and enjoy.

The opportunity presented itself in Week 16 against Arizona. The Seahawks' offense played its worst game of the season. So did Wilson. He passed for just 108 yards and completed 41 percent of his attempts, both season lows.

The kick to the groin came in the second quarter, when the Seattle defense gift-wrapped the ball at the Arizona 2. All the Seahawks had to do was punch it in. They couldn't. Instead, they sent kicker Steven Hauschka onto the field. He missed for only the second time this season.

The cameras snapped to Wilson on the sideline. His mouth tightened, ever so slightly. And then he stood

"I don't even know those words," Russell Wilson said before the 2013 season when asked about any possible sophomore slump.

By John Lok / The Seattle Times

"So very few guys could do what he's doing," Seahawks coach Pete Carroll said of Russell Wilson.

By Dean Rutz / The Seattle Times

there, stone-faced, the icy look we've come to expect.

The truths about Russell Wilson: He's fast. He's accurate.

He has big hands. He can make all the throws. He's poised. He works hard.

But here is where the perception of Wilson derails from the reality. All the time he spends studying defenses is not unique to NFL quarterbacks. What separates Wilson is that he's able to take what he studies and make it functional in the moment he needs it during a game.

"Russell doesn't get ambushed," said Dana Bible, his offensive coordinator at North Carolina State. "He's taking his play from Russell Wilson Quarterback 101 to Russell Wilson Quarterback 102 to Russell Wilson Quarterback 103. He's going through the different layers and scenarios that are waiting around the corner for him."

It was Bible, after all, who insisted before the season, "I'm telling you, if you think he was good in year one, just wait until year two. I've seen the growth. I'm just telling you, look out."

The NFL community waded in more cautiously. One successful year doesn't imply a fruitful career, and Wilson faced all the usual questions.

How would he hold up now that defenses had an offseason to study him? Would he fall victim to the sophomore slump?

Wilson shrugged. "I don't even know those words," he said before the season.

He answered his rookie year by throwing for more yards, more touchdowns and fewer interceptions.

Of all the strengths Wilson possesses, his freelancing is near the top. When a play breaks down, he's often at his best, and his scrambling can wear down defenders who think they have him, only to realize they do not.

His playmaking has bailed the Seahawks out many times this season, but there's a method to the madness. When it comes time to create, Wilson has thought through every possibility.

"When he's out there on the field, it looks instinctive," Bible said. "But I will argue that it's not instinctive. You're not going to surprise him. That's why when you watch him play he always looks so in control."

Even on his craziest plays, when he's zigzagging through defenders, he rarely looks choppy. Bible insists that's because Wilson covers so many scenarios before the game, he always has an escape route planned.

Seattle's receivers have specific assignments when Wilson takes off, and that can dictate where he goes. What looks like improv is more like a skit.

"It's like a play within a play," backup quarterback Tarvaris Jackson said.

Wilson's creativity was one of the most appealing parts of his game, but it was also vital to Seattle's success in 2013. He was one of the most pressured quarterbacks in the league behind a banged-up offensive line. When he lost his starting tackles and center because of injuries, Wilson's running ability went from an accessory to a necessity.

Playing behind three backup offensive linemen in Houston, Wilson faced heavy pressure all day. But come the fourth quarter and overtime, he burned the Texans with his legs when he realized he didn't have the time to sit back and throw.

"So very few guys could do what he's doing," Seahawks coach Pete Carroll said at one point this season.

In fact, as late as mid-November of the 2013 season, Wilson had yet to play a game in which the pocket consistently held up. That didn't happen until starting tackles Russell Okung and Breno Giacomini returned in the 11th game.

Against St. Louis on the road, Wilson had little time to throw, and passed for only 139 yards. But he didn't turn the ball over. He understood how the game was unfolding, and Seattle won 14-9.

"He trusted us on defense," safety Earl Thomas said, "and I love that about him."

Russell Wilson is mortal. He has bad games, no matter how much he prepares. Wilson's least productive games came against teams that were able to pressure him — Houston, St. Louis, San Francisco, Arizona. That is not a coincidence. Those teams have also had success because, for the most part, they've been able to keep Wilson in the pocket.

"He does change when he's hit early in the game," NFL Network analyst Bucky Brooks said, "but I think he's just like any other quarterback. When pressure begins to leak into the pocket, it changes them."

And yet Wilson has largely remained steady. As much as anything, he wanted to be consistent. He wanted to be reliable — what he calls the calm in the storm.

He wanted, in other words, to be the stone face on the sideline.

"Russell doesn't get ambushed," said Dana Bible, his offensive coordinator at North Carolina State. "He's taking his play from Russell Wilson Quarterback 101 to Russell Wilson Quarterback 102 to Russell Wilson Quarterback 103. He's going through the different layers and scenarios that are waiting around the corner for him."

By John Lok / The Seattle Times

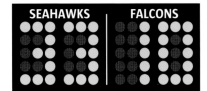

SEAHAWKS   FALCONS

REGULAR SEASON
> GAME 10
Nov. 10, 2013
SEAHAWKS @
FALCONS

GOING TO A HIGHER LEVEL

Hawks dominate in Atlanta with most complete game yet

By BOB CONDOTTA | *Seattle Times staff reporter*

A s the Seahawks quieted the Georgia Dome, they also sent maybe their loudest message yet about what this season can be.

"It's a great statement across the board," Seattle coach Pete Carroll said after the Seahawks ran through, passed over and shut down Atlanta, 33-10, in a rematch of their divisional playoff loss to the Falcons in Atlanta in January 2013.

Indeed, Carroll and many of Seattle's players later called it their most complete game of the season as they led from start to finish, gained a season-high 490 yards, (including 211 rushing, their second-most this year) and held Atlanta to 226, the third-fewest they have allowed.

The blowout came in the wake of two closer-than-expected wins over St. Louis and Tampa Bay, performances that the Seahawks realized were good enough for now, but not good enough to achieve

Jermaine Kearse came down with this 43-yard touchdown reception in the second quarter after a bit of trickery by the Seahawks. Marshawn Lynch took a pitch and ran left before passing back to Russell Wilson, who hit Kearse in the end zone.

By John Lok / The Seattle Times

Player Of The Game

Running back Marshawn Lynch rushed for 145 yards, setting a season-high for the second straight game. He averaged 6.0 yards a carry and scored the team's final touchdown. Lynch also had three catches for 16 yards.

Chris Clemons, top, and the Seahawks' defense frustrated quarterback Matt Ryan and the Falcons, holding them to 226 net yards of offense.

By John Lok / The Seattle Times

Game statistics

Seattle ...... 3　20　3　7 — 33
Atlanta ..... 0　3　7　0 — 10

FIRST QUARTER
Sea—Hauschka 39 FG, 7:32. Drive: 11 plays, 48 yards, 5:58.

SECOND QUARTER
Sea—Hauschka 43 FG, 11:53. Drive: 7 plays, 34 yards, 2:56.
Atl—Bryant 53 FG, 6:30. Drive: 10 plays, 45 yards, 5:23.
Sea—Kearse 43 pass from Wilson (Hauschka kick), 5:33. Drive: 2 plays, 80 yards, 0:57.
Sea—Hauschka 44 FG, 1:52. Drive: 5 plays, 49 yards, 2:01.
Sea—Tate 6 pass from Wilson (Hauschka kick), 0:01. Drive: 7 plays, 60 yards, 1:02.

THIRD QUARTER
Sea—Hauschka 53 FG, 7:49. Drive: 12 plays, 45 yards, 7:11.
Atl—Johnson 12 pass from Ryan (Bryant kick), 1:02. Drive: 13 plays, 82 yards, 6:47.

FOURTH QUARTER
Sea—Lynch 1 run (Hauschka kick), 8:48. Drive: 12 plays, 80 yards, 7:14.
Attendance: 70,309.

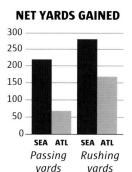

NET YARDS GAINED

SEA ATL — *Passing yards*
SEA ATL — *Rushing yards*

FIRST DOWNS

SEA 25
ATL 16

12 Rushing **3**
12 Passing **9**
1 Penalties **4**

TIME OF POSSESSION

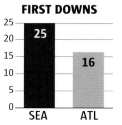

24:30 ATL
35:30 SEA

---

their lofty goals — games that Carroll said led to a little bit of soul-searching during the week.

"And the guys answered the call," Carroll said.

Seattle scored on seven of its first eight drives and blew the game open with a 17-point explosion in the final 5:33 of the first half that included a highlight-reel double-pass touchdown from Russell Wilson to Jermaine Kearse, and a similarly memorable one-handed scoring grab by Golden Tate.

They then put it away with a grinding second half in which Marshawn Lynch gained 78 of his season-high 145 yards while the defense ensured the Falcons never made it a game.

"Although last week we were 8-1, we felt like we could play so much better," said Tate, who led Seattle with 106 yards receiving on six catches. "And we still feel like we can play so much better, and I think that's important."

Seattle's defense, after allowing 405 yards rushing combined against the Rams and Bucs, held Atlanta to 64. It stifled Steven Jackson, who had just 11 yards on nine carries.

Linebacker K.J. Wright said Carroll held "a little private meeting" with the defense this week in which he told the players that "this run thing, it's got to get

corrected. ... Let's get this done and show who we are."

Safety Earl Thomas said the tough love was welcomed.

"Of course," he said. "Because the coaches expect a lot out of us, and they should. We have a great group, so you definitely want to take advantage of this opportunity because you never know what could happen next year or whenever."

Seattle also got four field goals from Steven Hauschka. His first two kicks made it 6-0 before the Falcons managed their only scoring drive of the first half to cut the lead to 6-3 with 6:30 to play in the second quarter.

Lynch, though, then brought Seattle to the Atlanta 43 with a 37-yard run. On the next play, he took a pitch out and ran left before passing back to Wilson, who found Kearse in the end zone.

Wilson said an earlier pitch out to Lynch had convinced them the play would work.

"The key was the run sell," Wilson said. "You've got

to sell the run — it doesn't work if you don't do that."

Atlanta then punted and Seattle responded with Hauschka's third field goal.

Atlanta punted again on its next possession and Tate returned it from the Seattle 8 to the 40 with 1:03 left. Seattle reached the 6-yard line with eight seconds left. On third down, Wilson threw to Tate on a fade route, who cradled the ball in with one hand while getting both feet barely in bounds.

That made it 23-3, and more than a few among the listed attendance of 70,309 headed out for a sunny afternoon, never to return.

"It was a great finish to the first half," Carroll said.

After an Atlanta touchdown made it 26-10 in the third quarter, the Seahawks then unveiled the type

of drive they have talked about wanting to see for weeks now — a 12-play, 80-yard march that included 11 runs, capped by a 1-yard scoring jaunt by Lynch.

And when it was over, Seattle was 9-1 for the first time in franchise history. Just as important, the Seahawks felt they played a game worthy of their lofty standing.

"That's really what the approach and the language was about," Carroll said. "That we are ready to step up to this level of play."

Byron Maxwell, top, celebrates with fellow defensive back Walter Thurmond after Thurmond took his first career interception 29 yards for a touchdown in the fourth quarter. Maxwell would play a crucial role down the stretch as Seattle lost players in the secondary due to injury and suspensions.

By John Lok / The Seattle Times

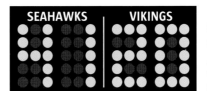

SEAHAWKS   VIKINGS

REGULAR SEASON
> GAME 11
Nov. 17, 2013
VIKINGS @
SEAHAWKS

RISE TO THE TOP

Seahawks own NFL's best record after dismantling the Vikings

By **BOB CONDOTTA** | *Seattle Times staff reporter*

With 15 days until their next game, the Seahawks will scatter, the bye week giving everyone a few days to return home.

"I'm going to get back in the country, man," said safety Earl Thomas, who plans to head back to his native Orange, Texas. "This is too much city for me right now. Got to get back to my roots and enjoy my family."

But the path to what the team hopes is its ultimate destination seemed clearer than ever after a feel-good 41-20 win over the Minnesota Vikings in front of 68,235 at CenturyLink Field.

Seattle's 13th win in a row at home set a team record and left the Seahawks with the best record in the NFL at 10-1, 1½ games ahead of the Saints for the best record in the NFC and 3½ games ahead of the 49ers in the NFC West.

"I think our expectations have been exceeded, actually," said receiver Doug Baldwin. "But we've got a long ways to go, obviously. We want to get to playing in February (in the Super Bowl)."

That seemed as realistic as ever after the Seahawks dominated in just about every way imaginable against the Vikings. To cite only a few highlights:

Player Of The Game

Russell Wilson had an efficient game, completing 13 of 18 pass attempts for 230 yards and two touchdowns with no interceptions in a little more than three quarters of work.

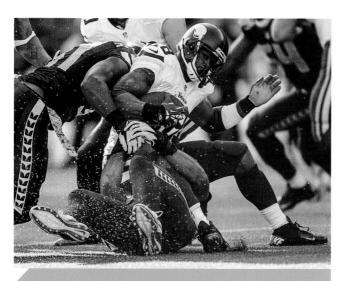

Adrian Peterson was held to 65 yards rushing by Seattle. In a game that featured Peterson and Marshawn Lynch, Vikings backup Toby Gerhart led all rushers with 67 yards.

By Dean Rutz / The Seattle Times

Game statistics

Minnesota ..... 3 10 0 7— 20
Seattle .... 10 14 0 17— 41

FIRST QUARTER

Sea—Hauschka 50 FG, 11:25. Drive: 5 plays, 1 yards, 2:04.

Min—Walsh 32 FG, 4:40. Drive: 13 plays, 66 yards, 6:45.

Sea—Lynch 4 run (Hauschka kick), 0:00. Drive: 4 plays, 78 yards, 2:10.

SECOND QUARTER

Min—Wright 38 pass from Ponder (Walsh kick), 11:28. Drive: 6 plays, 80 yards, 3:32.

Sea—Lynch 1 run (Hauschka kick), 6:26. Drive: 9 plays, 79 yards, 5:02.

Min—Walsh 45 FG, 0:48. Drive: 11 plays, 44 yards, 5:38.

Sea—Baldwin 19 pass from Wilson (Hauschka kick), 0:10. Drive: 5 plays, 46 yards, 0:38.

FOURTH QUARTER

Sea—Lynch 6 pass from Wilson (Hauschka kick), 13:14. Drive: 2 plays, 18 yards, 0:39.

Sea—Thurmond 29 interception return (Hauschka kick), 12:30.

Sea—Hauschka 26 FG, 10:12. Drive: 4 plays, 7 yards, 1:28.

Min—Wright 21 pass from Cassel (Walsh kick), 2:18. Drive: 7 plays, 60 yards, 2:53.

Attendance: 68,235.

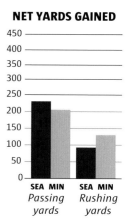

NET YARDS GAINED

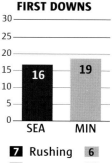

FIRST DOWNS

	7 Rushing	6
	9 Passing	10
	0 Penalties	3

TIME OF POSSESSION

34:09 MIN · 25:51 SEA

• Receiver Percy Harvin, making his Seahawks debut, showed what all the fuss has been about with a highlight-reel, one-handed catch to set up one touchdown in the second quarter and a 58-yard kickoff return to set up another. He touched the ball only those two times, but it proved more than enough on this day.

• Russell Wilson, working behind his starting offensive line for only the second full game this season, completed 13 of 18 passes for 230 yards and had a career-high passer rating of 151.4.

• Marshawn Lynch matched his season high with three touchdowns, including one on a somewhat-improvised toss from Wilson.

• The defense held Adrian Peterson to 65 yards on 21 carries while also forcing four turnovers, including Walter Thurmond's 29-yard interception return for a touchdown in the fourth quarter.

Coach Pete Carroll was so excited after the win that he said he'd rather the Seahawks didn't have a bye right now.

"I don't think it comes at a great time because we'd like to keep playing, to tell you the truth," Carroll said.

Seattle seemed ready from the beginning of this one, unlike more sluggish efforts a few weeks ago that resulted in close shaves against the Rams and Buccaneers.

Cliff Avril forced a Christian Ponder fumble on Minnesota's first possession that led to a field goal, and a Lynch touchdown run put Seattle up 10-3 at the end of the first quarter.

After the lone moment of angst — Ponder's 38-yard touchdown to Jarius Wright early in the second quarter that tied the game at 10 — Harvin made his official hello to Seattle.

On a third-and-10 play, he reeled in a Wilson pass with one hand for a 17-yard gain to put Seattle at the Minnesota 39 with 8:50 left.

That led to a Lynch touchdown run that put Seattle ahead for good, 17-10.

After a Minnesota field goal, Harvin made his debut as a kick returner. Carroll had planned to ease Harvin — who hadn't played since Nov. 4, 2012, when he was with Minnesota and missed the first 10 games this season after having hip surgery Aug. 1,

2013 — back into action, and wanted to hold him out of returning kickoffs.

But with regular returner Jermaine Kearse out with a concussion, Harvin got his chance and returned it 58 yards.

"I just wanted to stay calm and just play within the system and let the plays come to me," Harvin said.

That set up a Wilson-to-Baldwin 19-yard pass that made it 24-13 Seattle at halftime — tying the most points the Seahawks have scored in a half this season.

After a scoreless third quarter, Seattle turned it into a rout with 17 points in a span of 3:02 — all set up, or scored, by interceptions.

That's when the proverbial dam was destroyed, Thomas said.

"It broke," he said. "Water, it flooded. I was sad they took me out of the game at the end because you want to be part of that quarter."

Thomas and the Seahawks, though, know they now have a great chance to be part of something even bigger.

Their next game is against the New Orleans Saints, one that gives Seattle a chance to take a commanding lead in the race for playoff home-field advantage in the NFC.

"We are in a great position right now," Baldwin said. "We've been able to endure the adversity and the obstacles that we had to face earlier in the season with the injuries. Now we're getting healthy, and it's going to be a fun ride."

The Seahawks' Byron Maxwell, left, swipes the ball away from the Saints' Marques Colston, who had only four catches for 27 yards. Seattle's secondary held quarterback Drew Brees to 147 yards, his lowest total since 2006.

By Dean Rutz / The Seattle Times

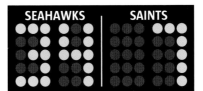

SEAHAWKS   SAINTS

REGULAR SEASON
> GAME 12
Dec. 2, 2013
SAINTS @
SEAHAWKS

KINGS OF THE NFC

Hawks virtually secure home-field advantage after blowing out the Saints

By BOB CONDOTTA | *Seattle Times staff reporter*

The showdown for NFC supremacy turned instead into a showcase for the Seahawks. And in the process of all-but-clinching home-field advantage in the NFC throughout the playoffs with a dominating 34-7 victory over the New Orleans Saints, the Seahawks also sent another loud message about their place atop the NFL hierarchy, just in case their league-best 11-1 record hadn't already said enough.

"We knew it's 'Monday Night Football' and a big stage and we had to come out and just make a statement and put on a show," said linebacker K.J. Wright.

That they did with a start-to-finish domination in front of a record crowd of 68,387 at CenturyLink Field that also set another Guinness noise record. The victory also officially clinched a playoff berth.

Seattle now has a two-game lead on the Saints and Carolina Panthers, who at 9-3 are the two

Player Of The Game

Quarterback Russell Wilson was 22-for-30 passing for 310 yards and three touchdowns. It was his first 300-yard passing game since the season opener and he also improved to 14-0 at home in his career.

Zach Miller hauled in a 2-yard touchdown pass late in the first quarter to stake the Seahawks to a 17-0 lead. Miller caught a 60-yard pass earlier on the drive.

By John Lok / The Seattle Times

Game statistics

New Orleans 0 7 0 0 — 7
Seattle   17 10 7 0 — 34

FIRST QUARTER

Sea — Hauschka 26 FG, 7:47.
Drive: 11 plays, 61 yards, 5:44.

Sea — Bennett 22 fumble return (Hauschka kick), 6:27.

Sea — Miller 2 pass from Wilson (Hauschka kick), 1:55. Drive: 6 plays, 73 yards, 2:58.

SECOND QUARTER

NO — Graham 2 pass from Brees (Hartley kick), 8:45.
Drive: 13 plays, 80 yards, 8:10.

Sea — Hauschka 20 FG, 3:41.
Drive: 10 plays, 82 yards, 5:04.

Sea — Baldwin 4 pass from Wilson (Hauschka kick), 0:13.
Drive: 12 plays, 88 yards, 1:52.

THIRD QUARTER

Sea — Coleman 8 pass from Wilson (Hauschka kick), 7:07.
Drive: 8 plays, 79 yards, 3:47.

Attendance: 68,387.

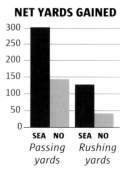

NET YARDS GAINED

FIRST DOWNS

SEA 23 NO 12

6 Rushing 2
14 Passing 7
3 Penalties 3

TIME OF POSSESSION

26:22 NO   33:38 SEA

closest pursuers in the NFC with four games to play.

But having already beaten both, the Seahawks have what is essentially a three-game lead in the NFC, and seem almost assured of being at home for the playoffs.

Wright, whose role in defending New Orleans tight end Jimmy Graham was key in the Seahawks allowing the Saints just 147 passing yards — the Saints' fewest since 2010 — said the stakes of the game weren't really on anyone's mind as it was being played.

But once it was over, Wright said the implications began to sink in.

"If we get home field in the playoffs, it's going to be real, real bad for other teams," Wright said.

That sounds more like fact than boast after the way the Seahawks toyed with the Saints in a highly hyped game that was never in doubt.

The Seahawks used a flurry of big plays on both sides of the ball to jump on the Saints early and often, grabbing leads of 17-0 at the end of the first quarter and 27-7 at halftime.

From there, they cruised to their seventh consecutive victory this season.

Seattle scored on all four of its first-half possessions in the first half — two touchdowns on passes from Russell Wilson and two Steven Haus-

chka field goals — and also got a 22-yard return of a fumble by Michael Bennett for a TD to blow the game open early.

Given the opponent and setting, it was Seattle's best half of the season as the Seahawks had 315 yards to just 90 for the Saints, who came in allowing 309.9 and gaining 415 per game, each among the top five in the NFL.

For the game, Seattle had 429 yards total offense to 188 for New Orleans.

Wilson, 22 of 30 for 310 yards, said he saw it coming.

"I texted coach (Pete) Carroll on Sunday and said the way we practiced this week is the best we have ever had," Wilson said. "So that preparation was big and I really think it showed up tonight."

That preparation was never more apparent than on one of the game's defining plays, a 52-yard pass from Wilson to Doug Baldwin on a third-down play after the Saints had cut the lead to 17-7. The play, that set up a Seattle field goal, was one

of a handful of times the Seahawks caught the Saints in a blitz.

"Throughout the week we saw some things on tape that we wanted to take advantage of," Baldwin said. "We knew (Saints defensive coordinator) Rob Ryan was a different coordinator in that he runs some different coverages in the open field that just aren't normal, yet at the same time he brings pressure."

Seattle, though, moved at will from the beginning. A 61-yard drive on the opening possession led to a Hauschka field goal.

The game began to turn for good when on the Saints' next drive, New Orleans faced a third-and-five on its own 25. Seattle defensive end Cliff Avril knocked the ball away from Saints quarterback Drew Brees before he threw it and it landed in the hands of Bennett, who caught it at the 22 and returned it for a touchdown to make it 10-0.

"Obviously, those are plays that swing games," said Saints coach Sean Payton.

On Seattle's next drive, Wilson rolled out right on a play-action pass and hit Zach Miller for 60 yards on a third-and-one play. That set up a 2-yard touchdown throw to Miller that made it 17-0.

Proof that it was simply Seattle's night came midway through the third quarter when a Wilson pass deflected off the hands of tight end Kellen Davis and directly to Derrick Coleman, who caught it and dived into the end zone to make it 34-7.

"Well, we had a blast tonight," Carroll said. "Just a really good night."

Russell Wilson was stripped on this first-quarter play by the 49ers NaVorro Bowman, though Seattle retained possession. But it was that kind of day for Wilson, who passed for 199 yards and was sacked twice.

By John Lok / The Seattle Times

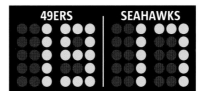

| 49ERS | SEAHAWKS |

REGULAR SEASON
> GAME 13

Dec. 8, 2013
SEAHAWKS @
49ERS

KEPT AT BAY

Seahawks fail to clinch NFC West, getting edged by 49ers

By **BOB CONDOTTA** | *Seattle Times staff reporter*

It was all there for the Seahawks in San Francisco — a chance to win the division title on the home turf of the defending champs (and their most heated rival) and send a message that the balance of power in the NFC West had changed for good.

But then, just like 49ers running back Frank Gore, it slipped away.

Gore's 51-yard dash set up Phil Dawson's 22-yard field goal with 26 seconds left that gave the 49ers a 19-17 win over the Seahawks at Candlestick Park. The loss ended a seven-game Seattle winning streak and dropped the Seahawks to 11-2 while the 49ers improved to 9-4.

"The game came right to us," said Seattle coach Pete Carroll. "We had a chance and we just let them get out with the big run and that was it. It was a one-play deal as it came down to it."

While the Seahawks were, as receiver Doug Baldwin said, "extremely disappointed," they said they realized everything remains out there for them.

"We would have loved to get the win, but it

Player Of The Game

Golden Tate came up with another big punt return, taking one 38 yards to the San Francisco 27 with less than 10 minutes left in the game. The good field position eventually led to a field goal that gave Seattle its last lead. Tate also had a team-high six catches for 65 yards.

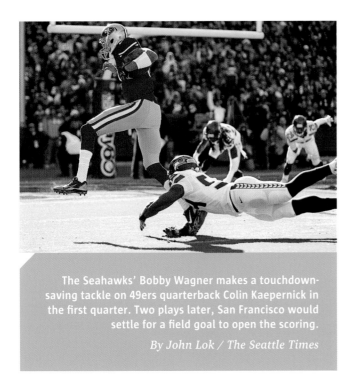

The Seahawks' Bobby Wagner makes a touchdown-saving tackle on 49ers quarterback Colin Kaepernick in the first quarter. Two plays later, San Francisco would settle for a field goal to open the scoring.

By John Lok / The Seattle Times

Game statistics

Seattle	0 14 0 3	— 17
San Francisco	6 10 0 3	— 19

FIRST QUARTER

SF — Dawson 23 FG, 5:04. Drive: 10 plays, 56 yards, 4:44.

SF — Dawson 48 FG, 0:58. Drive: 4 plays, 4 yards, 0:54.

SECOND QUARTER

Sea — Lynch 11 run (Hauschka kick), 12:17. Drive: 8 plays, 80 yards, 3:41.

SF — Dawson 52 FG, 7:56. Drive: 10 plays, 40 yards, 4:21.

Sea — Willson 39 pass from Wilson (Hauschka kick), 3:47. Drive: 7 plays, 72 yards, 4:09.

SF — Davis 8 pass from Kaepernick (Dawson kick), 0:06. Drive: 9 plays, 72 yards, 3:41.

FOURTH QUARTER

Sea — Hauschka 31 FG, 6:20. Drive: 7 plays, 14 yards, 2:57.

SF — Dawson 22 FG, 0:26. Drive: 11 plays, 76 yards, 5:54.

Attendance: 69,732.

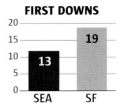

NET YARDS GAINED

SEA SF — Passing yards
SEA SF — Rushing yards

FIRST DOWNS

13 — SEA
19 — SF

1	Rushing	**8**
11	Passing	**9**
1	Penalties	**2**

TIME OF POSSESSION

32:28 SF — 27:32 SEA

---

doesn't change anything for us," said cornerback Richard Sherman. Indeed, Seattle still needs to win two of its last three games to take not only the NFC West but home-field advantage in the NFC playoffs.

"I didn't feel like the season was going to end one way or another today," Carroll said. "And it's not."

In fact, some of the Seahawks said that the result might in a way be good for a team that has already clinched a playoff berth and hadn't really played a close game since beating Tampa Bay in overtime on Nov. 3, and hadn't lost since a 34-28 loss at Indianapolis on Oct. 6.

"Not that we were cocky in any way, but being able to face this adversity is only going to help us further down the line when we are in the playoffs because we are probably going to have a game like this coming up shortly," Baldwin said. "It's going to build character. We haven't had a tough game in recent weeks. So I think you try to take positives out of negatives and the only positive we can take out of this is that it's going to make us stronger for later down the line."

The specific lesson Sunday concerned penalties, a seasonlong bugaboo that reared its head a bit too often against the 49ers. Seattle had nine

penalties for 85 yards, two of which gave the 49ers first downs on drives on which they later scored.

"We expected to blow them out, but they got the benefit of a few calls throughout the game," Sherman said.

Seattle came into the day averaging eight penalties per game, with Baldwin noting that "we are good enough to overcome the penalties that we had. But we are also good enough to not have those penalties. When you are playing a team like the San Francisco 49ers, you can't have those mistakes."

Otherwise, Carroll said the game was largely what he expected it would be — a "good, hard-fought game. Kind of a slugfest is what it felt like."

Indeed, the game featured six lead changes as each team struggled to gain the upper hand. In that regard, it was completely different from the last two meetings in Seattle, won by the Seahawks by a combined score of 71-16.

Baldwin felt that the 49ers — who were playing with a little more desperation with a playoff spot still not secured — came out "with a little bit more energy than we had in the first quarter."

Two Dawson field goals gave the 49ers a 6-0

lead at the end of the first quarter. Seattle, though, responded with touchdown drives of 80 and 72 yards to take a 14-9 lead late in the second quarter after Dawson hit another field goal. The touchdowns came via an 11-yard Marshawn Lynch run and a 39-yard pass from Russell Wilson to rookie tight end Luke Willson.

The 49ers, though, scored their lone touchdown with six seconds left in the half on an 8-yard pass from Colin Kaepernick to Vernon Davis to take a 16-14 halftime lead.

There was no more scoring until a 31-yard Steven Hauschka field goal, set up by a 38-yard punt return by Golden Tate, put Seattle ahead 17-16 with 6:20 left.

But after one 49ers first down, Gore took a handoff to the left and then cut back into the open before falling down at the Seattle 18.

"We just got outplayed on the play," Carroll said. "They blocked us really nicely and they took

advantage of it."

One more first down, on a Kaepernick 8-yard run on third-and-seven, allowed the 49ers to run down the clock before Dawson's field goal. Carroll said he debated letting the 49ers score so Seattle would be assured of some time left on the clock to try to win or tie it.

Seattle, instead, was in desperation mode when it got the ball back with 21 seconds left, and a deep Wilson pass was intercepted by Eric Wright to end the game.

"We are still in a great position like we want to be," said safety Earl Thomas. "We are just going to move on."

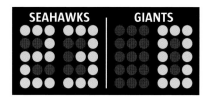

SEAHAWKS GIANTS

REGULAR SEASON
> GAME 14

Dec. 15, 2013
SEAHAWKS @
GIANTS

ZERO HOUR

*Hawks post shutout in New Jersey
with hopes to return*

By BOB CONDOTTA | *Seattle Times staff reporter*

It didn't matter that Richard Sherman wasn't really certain which teammate was behind him.

What mattered was that he knew for sure one of his teammates was there.

"I know that Earl (Thomas) or Kam (Chancellor) are on their way," Sherman said. "At all times, they are speeding somewhere in the vicinity."

So when Eli Manning lofted a pass toward Hakeem Nicks in the corner of the end zone with 4:24 left Sunday, Sherman confidently tipped the ball back in play, where Thomas swooped in to grab it.

And when he did, he preserved Seattle's first shutout of the season, a 23-0 win over the Giants at MetLife Stadium in East Rutherford, N.J., that pushed the Seahawks closer to clinching all of their regular-season goals.

Because the 49ers beat Tampa Bay 33-14, the Seahawks could not clinch the NFC West title outright. But thanks to New Orleans' loss to the Rams, all the Seahawks need is to win one of their

Player Of The Game

Cornerback Byron Maxwell intercepted two passes as part of a defensive effort that produced the first shutout of the season for Seattle. Maxwell's second interception, early in the fourth quarter, led to Seattle's final touchdown.

The Giants' Prince Amukamara was no match for the Seahawks' Marshawn Lynch on this first-quarter play. Lynch only had 47 yards rushing, but led Seattle in receiving yards with 73.

By John Lok / The Seattle Times

Golden Tate, here making a 17-yard reception, was the Seahawks' leading receiver in 2013, finishing the season with 64 receptions for 898 yards.

By John Lok / The Seattle Times

Game statistics

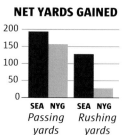

Seattle	3	10	3	7 —	23
New York	0	0	0	0 —	0

FIRST QUARTER
Sea—Hauschka 49 FG, 8:33.
Drive: 5 plays, 11 yards, 2:00.

SECOND QUARTER
Sea—Lynch 2 run (Hauschka kick), 5:30. Drive: 7 plays, 62 yards, 3:33.

Sea—Hauschka 44 FG, 0:03.
Drive: 10 plays, 40 yards, 2:45.

THIRD QUARTER
Sea—Hauschka 24 FG, 8:47.
Drive: 9 plays, 39 yards, 4:03.

FOURTH QUARTER
Sea—Baldwin 12 pass from Wilson (Hauschka kick), 12:13.
Drive: 6 plays, 16 yards, 2:40.

Attendance: 79,691.

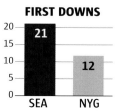

NET YARDS GAINED

SEA NYG — *Passing yards* SEA NYG — *Rushing yards*

FIRST DOWNS

SEA 21   NYG 12

9	Rushing	1
11	Passing	10
1	Penalties	1

TIME OF POSSESSION

26:02 NYG   33:58 SEA

last two home games to claim the division title and home-field advantage throughout the playoffs (one 49ers loss, to either Atlanta or at Arizona, would also do the trick).

And assuming they get that done, the Seahawks will become even stronger favorites to return to MetLife Stadium for Super Bowl XLVIII on Feb. 2.

"It's a beautiful place," Sherman said with a smile. "And we'd love to be back."

After a 19-17 loss at San Francisco that put a little bit of urgency back into their remaining schedule, the Seahawks played a game as complete as any this season.

The Giants didn't cross midfield until there was 7:08 left in the game and managed just 181 yards, the fewest allowed by the Seahawks this season.

The Giants had just 25 yards rushing on 14 carries, the fewest allowed by the Seahawks since holding the Rams to 17 on Dec. 17, 2002.

"We didn't block anybody," grumbled Giants coach Tom Coughlin after his team fell to 5-9. "We didn't make any plays."

Seattle's defense also had five interceptions — two each by Sherman and Byron Maxwell — and forced the Giants to punt on each of their other eight possessions.

Sherman said the defense was motivated by a few comments it heard from the Giants during the week, including one from Manning in which he noted how Sherman likes to "get his hands on the receivers" and that the Giants would "try to take advantage of his style of play."

"Eli said we are over-aggressive and that they were going to take advantage of that," Sherman said. "And I think we showed him we are over-aggressive, but it's hard to take advantage of it. It's easier said than done."

Manning's five interceptions gave him 25 for the season, most in the NFL.

The offense, meanwhile, shook off a sluggish start (four punts on their first five possessions) to score on five of six possessions from the middle of the second quarter until early in the fourth.

"We had a terrific football game today," gushed coach Pete Carroll. "Really loved the way we played across the board. … everybody hit, ran hard and played tough football the way we want to do it."

Russell Wilson threw one touchdown pass, becoming only the third player in history to throw for 50 or more in his first two seasons (Dan Ma-

rino and Peyton Manning are the others). He also led Seattle with 50 yards rushing as the Seahawks had 134 on the ground.

Running back Marshawn Lynch and receiver Doug Baldwin each had six receptions as Wilson hit seven different players in going 18 of 27 for 206 yards.

It was the defense that carried the day, though. At the end of the first half, Manning threw a desperation heave near the Seattle goal line that either Thomas or Sherman could have picked off. Thomas relented and let Sherman get it — his second of the day and sixth of the season, putting him in a tie for the NFL lead — then reminded him of it as they headed off the field.

"That's what you do for your brother," Thomas said. "And when you do good things like that, the ball always comes back and finds you."

The Giants' longest drive through the first three quarters was 29 yards, none lasting more than five plays. Midway through the fourth quarter, it took a personal foul on Chancellor on a completed pass to finally get New York past midfield.

The shutout seemed doomed when the Giants got to the Seattle 13 a few plays later. But on second down came the Manning pass to Nicks and Sherman's tip. As Thomas had predicted, the ball did indeed come back and find him, bringing with it a much-desired shutout.

"I tried to tip it up with enough air for someone to get under it," Sherman said. "And Earl got under it. I owed him one."

Doug Baldwin's near-catch against the Cardinals' Jerraud Powers epitomized the Seahawks' performance in a game they could never get within their grasp.

By Bettina Hansen / The Seattle Times

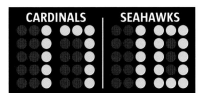

CARDINALS   SEAHAWKS

REGULAR SEASON
> GAME 15

Dec. 22, 2013
CARDINALS @
SEAHAWKS

PUT ON HOLD

Hawks lose at CenturyLink for first time since 2011; West title still in play

By **BOB CONDOTTA** | *Seattle Times staff reporter*

After a defeat as disheartening and surprising as any they have experienced together, the Seattle Seahawks said they will now try to do what their offense never really could — move forward.

"It won't be difficult," said safety Earl Thomas in the quiet of the locker room after a 17-10 loss to Arizona. "Because everything you want is still right in front of your face."

Indeed, all that Seattle was playing for — a chance to clinch the NFC West and home-field advantage throughout the playoffs — the Seahawks can still attain.

But now, they need either the San Francisco 49ers to lose one more game or to beat the St. Louis Rams at CenturyLink Field in the regular-season finale.

"I was going to tell them they had to win that game no matter what anyway," said Seattle coach Pete Carroll. "So here we go."

Player Of The Game

Safety Kam Chancellor followed up his strong play against the Giants by leading the Seahawks in tackles with 11. Chancellor also came up with an interception in the end zone on Arizona's opening possession.

To do so, though, they'll have to figure out how to jump-start an offense that never found its gear against the Cardinals.

Seattle was held to 192 yards, the second-lowest total of the season, finishing with a season-low 89 net yards passing.

The Seahawks also couldn't get much consistent running against an Arizona team that entered the game ranked first in the NFL in rushing defense. Seattle had 103 yards, but only 52 on 13 carries in the final three quarters.

"We did not get the movement that we wanted," Carroll said. "All in all, they did a better job than we did."

Still, Seattle appeared in position to get the win anyway when Wilson hit Zach Miller with an 11-yard touchdown pass with 7:26 remaining to take a 10-9 lead.

For the second time in three games, though, the defense couldn't hold a late, slim lead — the 49ers drove for a last-minute field goal to win 19-17 in San Francisco two games ago, to also deny Seattle a chance to win the NFC West and take home-field advantage.

This time, Arizona responded to the Miller touchdown with an 80-yard, 10-play drive capped by a 31-yard pass from Carson Palmer to Malcolm Floyd with 2:13 left.

The drive was keyed by a holding penalty on Seattle linebacker Malcolm Smith on a third-down play, one of nine penalties for 102 yards against the Seahawks (seven called on the defense).

On Seattle's first play of its next drive, a Wilson pass intended for Doug Baldwin was ruled to bounce off Baldwin's arm around midfield and into

Game statistics

Arizona	0	3	3	11 —	17
Seattle	0	3	0	7 —	10

SECOND QUARTER

Sea—Hauschka 27 FG, 13:42.
Drive: 13 plays, 70 yards, 6:02.

Ari—Feely 39 FG, 2:15. Drive:
16 plays, 75 yards, 8:21.

THIRD QUARTER

Ari—Feely 46 FG, 0:27. Drive: 6
plays, 27 yards, 3:03.

FOURTH QUARTER

Ari—Feely 26 FG, 10:39. Drive:
5 plays, 45 yards, 2:34.

Sea—Miller 11 pass from
Wilson (Hauschka kick), 7:26.
Drive: 6 plays, 61 yards, 3:13.

Ari—Flo 31 pass from Palmer
(Mendenhall run), 2:13. Drive:
10 plays, 80 yards, 5:13.

Attendance: 68,266.

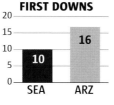

NET YARDS GAINED

FIRST DOWNS

	SEA	ARZ
First downs	10	16
Rushing	3	4
Passing	6	6
Penalties	1	6

TIME OF POSSESSION

37:24 ARZ — 22:36

Coach Pete Carroll and the Seahawks failed to clinch the NFC West and home-field advantage throughout the playoffs against the Cardinals, leaving it to the regular-season finale against the Rams. "I was going to tell them they had to win that game no matter what anyway. So here we go," Carroll said.

By John Lok / The Seattle Times

the air, where it was caught by Arizona linebacker Karlos Dansby. The play was upheld after the review, even though Baldwin insisted the ball hit the ground.

"Yeah, it hit the turf," Baldwin said, adding he knew because "I don't think anybody in the stadium had a better view of it than me."

The loss snapped Seattle's 14-game home winning streak, a franchise record, while dropping the Seahawks to 12-3. Arizona, meanwhile, improved to 10-5, having won seven of its last eight while also getting a measure of revenge for a 58-0 loss to Seattle at CenturyLink Field in December 2012.

Arizona also won despite four interceptions by Palmer, two in the end zone. Palmer threw three in the first half, the main reason the score was 3-3 at halftime despite Arizona dominating statistically. His final pick of the half was returned to the 3-yard line by Smith.

But indicative of the offense's struggles, Seattle gained only 2 yards on two runs, and then Wilson threw incomplete on third down. And then the normally sure-footed kicker Steven Hauschka — who entered the game having made 30 of 31 field goals for the season — clanked a 24-yard field goal off the upright.

"It just didn't happen for us today," Thomas said.

Some of what happened, though, perpetuated recent disturbing trends, such as penalties (Seattle came in having been flagged 112 times, most in the NFL) and an offense held to 50 points over the last three games.

Wilson said he wasn't too concerned about the passing game, saying, "I thought it was one of those games where we were just an inch off here or there, for whatever reason."

Baldwin credited a good scheme by Arizona that he said made it hard to discern what the Cardinals were doing.

"I've never had that difficult of a time trying to figure out what their coverages were in the back end," he said. "They did a hell of a job of disguising things. We would think they would be in man-to-man and they would flip it to zone ... it just didn't go the way we had planned for it to go."

Seattle also has lost two of three, games when it could have clinched the NFC West and home field.

"It's definitely not a time to panic," Thomas said. "We've just got to refocus ourselves and control what we can control. ... There are going to be games like this. Hopefully this is our last one."

In a near replay from their first matchup against the Rams, Golden Tate goes up to grab a pass in front of Janoris Jenkins before running the rest of the way to complete a 47-yard touchdown reception.

By Dean Rutz / The Seattle Times

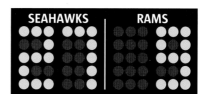

SEAHAWKS   RAMS

REGULAR SEASON
> GAME 16

Dec. 29, 2013
RAMS @
SEAHAWKS

GETTING THE JOB DONE

Hawks claim NFC's top record, home-field advantage in playoffs

By **BOB CONDOTTA** | *Seattle Times staff reporter*

The Rams tried to get inside their heads.

But when it ended, it was the Seahawks walking off the field wearing the crown they had been working for all season, their 27-9 win over St. Louis clinching the NFC West title and home-field advantage through the playoffs.

Seattle finished the regular season with a 13-3 record that tied the 2005 team for the best in franchise history, and got a bye the first weekend of the playoffs.

"It feels good," said safety Earl Thomas. "But we still have some work to do."

Indeed, it was a rather muted celebration in the locker room after Seattle's eighth division title, the second time the Seahawks have won home-field advantage in the playoffs. The other came in 2005, when Seattle won two home games to get to its only Super Bowl. This team hopes to duplicate that feat.

"We haven't done anything yet, in our opin-

Player Of The Game

Wide receiver Golden Tate finished with eight catches for 129 yards and a 47-yard touchdown catch. It was his second 100-yard receiving day of the season, with the other coming against Atlanta.

The Rams' Austin Pettis crashes into the Seahawks' Clint Gresham on a punt return in the fourth quarter. Seattle was stingy about allowing punt-return yards for most of 2013, allowing 82 yards in the regular season, 57 of those by the Rams in the regular-season finale.

By John Lok / The Seattle Times

Game statistics

St. Louis ...	0	0	3	6 —	9
Seattle	7	6	7	7 —	27

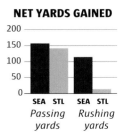

NET YARDS GAINED

FIRST QUARTER
Sea—Smith 37 interception return (Hauschka kick), 9:50.

SECOND QUARTER
Sea—Hauschka 28 FG, 6:14. Drive: 11 plays, 65 yards, 6:32.

Sea—Hauschka 35 FG, 0:03. Drive: 10 plays, 44 yards, 2:40.

THIRD QUARTER
StL—Zuerlein 36 FG, 10:49. Drive: 5 plays, 13 yards, 1:28.

Sea—Lynch 2 run (Hauschka kick), 2:21. Drive: 14 plays, 80 yards, 8:28.

FOURTH QUARTER
Sea—Tate 47 pass from Wilson (Hauschka kick), 9:14. Drive: 4 plays, 61 yards, 2:10.

StL—Cook 2 pass from Clemens (pass failed), 4:13. Drive: 13 plays, 71 yards, 5:01.

Attendance: 68,264.

FIRST DOWNS

SEA	STL
20	11

SEA		STL
7	Rushing	1
8	Passing	8
5	Penalties	2

TIME OF POSSESSION

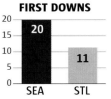

26:20 STL | 33:40 SEA

---

ion," said quarterback Russell Wilson. "Our goal every year is to win the NFC West, and that's our mindset, and so once we accomplish that we can check that off the list. But we still have a lot more to do."

The Seahawks got plenty of practice reining in their emotions during a sometimes-bizarre game that featured numerous bouts of pushing and shoving after the whistle. The Rams drew 12 penalties, including the ejection of defensive tackle Kendall Langford for making contact with an official in the third quarter.

The Seahawks said they knew that the Rams, playing out the string of their eventual 7-9 season, might try to turn the game into a literal slugfest.

"We understood coming into the game that they were going to do some crazy stuff," said linebacker Bobby Wagner. "We didn't know what. But we knew they didn't really have anything to play for with their season over. So we just had to keep our composure."

Seattle largely did that and focused on the task at hand, particularly a defense that held the Rams to just 13 yards rushing, tying a Seahawks

team record set in 1990 against Green Bay.

That marked a vast turnaround from Seattle's 14-9 win at St. Louis when the Rams rushed for 200.

"I knew they ran on us the first time," said Wagner, who led Seattle with 12 tackles. "I took it personal to make sure they didn't run on us again."

The defense also helped quell any early anxiety for a team that had lost in two earlier opportunities to sew up the West and home-field advantage. Linebacker Malcolm Smith picked off Kellen Clemens' pass on St. Louis' first possession and returned it 37 yards for a touchdown.

"I wasn't going to be three yards away this time," said Smith, who was stopped at the 3-yard line in the loss to Arizona, after which the Seahawks were unable to punch it in.

Added coach Pete Carroll: "The difference between this week and last week, you knock that one in."

Also different this week was an offense that was able to finally wear down the Rams.

Seattle led 13-0 at the half, adding two Steven Hauschka field goals in the second quarter. Still,

each felt like something of a defeat with the Seahawks unable to get in the end zone after getting inside the St. Louis 10.

After St. Louis used a 32-yard punt return to set up a field goal that made it 13-3, Seattle's running game and the Rams' testiness finally broke the game open. After Seattle had reached the St. Louis 23, four St. Louis personal fouls — including the ejection of Langford — moved the ball to 1. Marshawn Lynch scored on a 2-yard run two plays later to make it 20-3.

Early in the fourth quarter, Seattle could finally breathe easy after Wilson hit Golden Tate for a 47-yard touchdown in a play strikingly similar to the 80-yard hookup that beat the Rams in St. Louis. Each time, Tate ran a deep route down the sideline and then outmaneuvered St. Louis cornerback Janoris Jenkins to make the catch and race into the end zone.

This time, though, there was no taunting by Tate, only celebrating by the Seahawks, who had insisted all week that there was nothing to worry about despite the loss to the Cardinals.

"We know we had a couple shots at it earlier and didn't get that done, so it was frustrating," Carroll said. "When it came time to finish, we did it. Real proud of that."

So, too, were the players in the leave-no-doubt manner in which the win was accomplished.

"After last week's game, we wanted to send a message that even though we had a loss, it's still going to be hard to win here," Wagner said.

Golden Tate feels the affection of the fans after the Seahawks nailed down the top seed in the NFC, home-field advantage throughout the playoffs and the franchise's eighth division title.

By Bettina Hansen / The Seattle Times

RUSSELL WILSON
QUARTERBACK

KAM CHANCELLOR
SAFETY

RED BRYANT
DEFENSIVE END

SEAHAWKS PLANS
BY PETE CARROLL & JOHN SCHNEIDER

Blueprint for success

Seahawks aren't afraid to take chances – or quickly move on when they make a mistake

By JAYSON JENKS | *Seattle Times staff reporter*

The day the Seahawks drafted Russell Wilson — April 27, 2012 — general manager John Schneider was intense. "His head was about to explode," said former Seahawks owner John Nordstrom.

Schneider had fallen hard for Wilson. He liked him so much that he wanted to draft him in the second round before coach Pete Carroll talked him out of it.

The plan was to take Wilson in the third round.

Carroll and his staff liked Wilson, but Schneider loved him. "We were just trying to understand what he could see in a guy who was undersized at that position," offensive line coach Tom Cable says.

Football is a funny business. No one gets into it lacking ego. In fact, many people get into because they

The strong relationship between Seahawks general manager John Schneider, left, and coach Pete Carroll has been a key to the team's success. "Each of those guys wants to give the other credit. That never happens," former Seahawks owner John Nordstrom said.

By John Lok / The Seattle Times

have ego. And herein lies a question that can torpedo franchises: Where's the line between a healthy ego that fortifies your convictions and a prideful one that clouds judgment?

Schneider, of course, eventually netted Wilson in the third round with the 75th pick. But just as important is what happened next.

When Wilson arrived in Seattle, Carroll and his staff immediately saw why Schneider wanted him. The way he prepared, his ability to scramble and make all the throws, came alive.

Carroll holds the most power in the organization, and Seattle had signed free-agent quarterback Matt Flynn for $26 million the month before. But Carroll didn't blink. Shortly before the season, he named Wilson his starting quarterback.

One of the first things the Seahawks asked of Cable surprised him. Cable had agreed to become Seattle's offensive-line coach in 2011. Upon arriving in Seattle, Cable was asked to do something he'd never done before.

"Coming here, the first thing they said was, 'Would you go spend some time with the scouts and let them know what it is you're looking for? Describe the linemen you're looking for,'" Cable said. "And I was like, 'Heck yeah, I'll do that! That's awesome.'"

The Seahawks have become one of the NFL's best teams for a lot reasons, but many of them begin with little moments like that: Go talk to the scouts so they know what you're looking for.

That starts with Carroll and Schneider, the men tasked in 2010 with turning the Seahawks around.

"Each of those guys wants to give the other credit," Nordstrom says. "That never happens."

The byproduct is flexibility. Scouts and personnel people don't have to operate within rigid parameters, and the coaching staff is pliable enough to adapt their scheme. Whereas many teams are looking for a square peg to begin with, the Seahawks are willing to make the hole once they get the peg.

Red Bryant is one of Seattle's most interesting cases. In six seasons, he has never had more than 32 tackles or 1.5 sacks. Even his position — defensive end — is misleading because it conjures images of speed rushers hellbent on quarterbacks.

Bryant couldn't be further from that, and yet he's crucial to Seattle. He plays like a defensive tackle but lines up at defensive end. His job description is simple: Knock the guy in front of you backward and stop

teams from running your way.

Bryant is a square peg who was once jammed into a round hole. Only when Carroll arrived did he fit.

When Carroll arrived in 2010 — Bryant's third year — he retained defensive coordinator Dan Quinn, who had been Seattle's defensive-line coach under Jim Mora. Carroll's scheme requires a big defensive end capable of stuffing the run, and in Bryant he saw a perfect match.

The height (6 feet 4) and reach (36-inch arms) that led Bryant to struggle on the inside became an advantage against offensive tackles on the outside.

When Carroll and Schneider took over in 2010, the Seahawks were too slow, too old and too small.

Joe Pawelek was an undrafted linebacker in camp that year, and when the idea of Carroll and Schneider changing the culture is raised, he laughs.

"They weren't changing a culture," he says. "They were creating their own culture."

In that first season, the Seahawks made an astonishing 283 roster moves.

That revolving door set the tone for the way the organization would operate. Underneath the positive vibes and music at practices is a cutthroat tenacity.

The most obvious example is Flynn, but there are plenty of others. In 2013, the Seahawks cut rookie receiver Chris Harper, a fourth-round draft pick. He was one of the highest-drafted rookies released.

At one point during Earl Thomas' rookie season, Carroll approached his young safety with a warning.

"You know, Earl," Carroll told him in 2010, "I might have to sit you down because it's getting to the point where you don't know what you're going to do next."

Carroll didn't sit Thomas, but his message stuck. Thomas turned into a serious candidate for defensive player of the year.

Not long after Wilson was named the starter, Nordstrom told Carroll he admired his guts.

"Oh, no," Carroll responded. "This didn't take any guts. This was a no-brainer."

The reality is the Seahawks likely wouldn't have competed for a Super Bowl had they not drafted Wilson. As good as the defense is and as much as they run the ball, Wilson was the final piece. He is also emblematic of how the organization has come to power: a collaboration between a savvy front office, a coach willing to trust what he sees and, of course, a little luck.

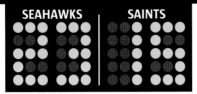

Running back Marshawn Lynch carried the load offensively for the Seahawks against the Saints, averaging five yards a carry and scoring twice, including on this 15-yard touchdown run early in the second quarter.

By John Lok / The Seattle Times

A STEP CLOSER

Defense, Lynch enable Hawks to hold on and advance to NFC Championship Game

By **BOB CONDOTTA** | *Seattle Times staff reporter*

Rain fell. Wind blew.

And the Saints came marching in hoping for a little revenge and a spot in the NFC title game.

When it finally ended, though, it was the Seahawks who were marching on to within a game of the Super Bowl, thanks to a 23-15 victory in front of a CenturyLink Field record crowd of 68,388.

And afterward, in a locker room that was happy but understanding that work remains, Seattle quarterback Russell Wilson reminded his teammates of just how close they are to the goal they set the minute they walked off the field in Atlanta the previous season.

"We've got 60 minutes left of football," Wilson said. "That's 60 minutes of your life. The

Player Of The Game

Running back Marshawn Lynch ran for 140 yards, a Seahawks postseason record, and accounted for both of Seattle's touchdowns.

Percy Harvin was tested for a concussion and pulled from the game in the second quarter. He missed all but one game during the 2013 regular season.

By Dean Rutz / The Seattle Times

Game statistics

	1	2	3	4		
New Orleans	0	0	0	15	—	15
Seattle	6	10	0	7	—	23

FIRST QUARTER

Sea — Hauschka 38 FG, 10:19. Drive: 6 plays, 20 yards, 3:20.

Sea — Hauschka 49 FG, 0:37. Drive: 9 plays, 34 yards, 4:26.

SECOND QUARTER

Sea — Lynch 15 run (Hauschka kick), 14:17. Drive: 2 plays, 24 yards, 0:34.

Sea — Hauschka 26 FG, 1:18. Drive: 12 plays, 63 yards, 4:44.

FOURTH QUARTER

NO — Robinson 1 run (Ingram run), 13:11. Drive: 9 plays, 74 yards, 4:27.

Sea — Lynch 31 run (Hauschka kick), 2:40. Drive: 4 plays, 62 yards, 1:11.

NO — Colston 9 pass from Brees (Graham kick), 0:26. Drive: 9 plays, 80 yards, 2:14.

Attendance: 68,388.

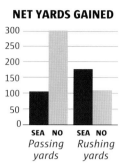

NET YARDS GAINED

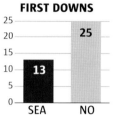

FIRST DOWNS

SEA 13   NO 25

6	Rushing	6
5	Passing	16
2	Penalties	3

TIME OF POSSESSION

30:30 NO   29:30 SEA

best 60 minutes you can possibly play and then you play in the Super Bowl. That's pretty awesome to think about."

And ultimately, that reality was all that really mattered on a day that began as a party and ended with some unexpected anxiety as the Saints three times in the fourth quarter had the ball with a chance to tie the score.

"This was an interesting finish to this game," said Seahawks coach Pete Carroll.

Seattle led 16-0 at half, seemingly on their way to another victory over the Saints as easy as the 34-7 beatdown the Seahawks gave them in the regular season.

Instead, the Saints finally began to creep back in as the Seahawks managed one first down in the third quarter.

Even after Marshawn Lynch's 31-yard touchdown run with 2:40 left put Seattle ahead 23-8 and seemed to seal it, the Saints created a little heartburn with a touchdown and then a recovery of an onside kick that slid through the hands of Seahawks receiver Golden Tate with 24 seconds left.

"That could have been bad," Tate said. "That could have been real bad."

The game, though, ended in somewhat fitting fashion for a mistake-prone Saints team — a penalty for an illegal forward pass on the final play.

Seattle won despite being outgained 409-277 in total yardage and with Wilson completing just 9 of 18 attempts for 103 yards on a day when the passing attack was at times conservative by design due to the elements, and then hamstrung by yet another injury to hard-luck receiver Percy Harvin, who left in the second quarter with a concussion in just his second game of the season.

Ultimately, Seattle won in the style Carroll prides himself on most — with defense and a solid running game.

While the Saints' Drew Brees ended up with 309 passing yards, only 34 came in the first half as the Seahawks grabbed a lead they would never relinquish. The defense helped set up Seattle's first touchdown by forcing a New Orleans fumble at the 24.

"It's as complete a defense as there is in the league," Brees said of the Seahawks.

Michael Bennett, in particular, played with a relentlessness that defined his tenure in Seattle, especially in the last few weeks. Time and again, he came at Brees and forced him to either get rid of the ball or move in the pocket.

At times against the Saints, during TV time-outs when both teams were idle on the field, Bennett stood at the line of scrimmage and started yelling at the New Orleans' offensive line as they walked to the ball.

His message: "They're not good," he recalled, "and we're better than them."

"That's just how he is," defensive tackle Bran-

A crowd of 68,388, a CenturyLink Field record, braved the wind and rain to watch the Seahawks win their sixth consecutive home playoff game.

By Bettina Hansen / The Seattle Times

Two field goals by Steven Hauschka, who had little trouble kicking through the wind and the rain, gave Seattle a 6-0 lead at the end of the first quarter. Hauschka's second kick came after his counterpart, Shayne Graham, missed a 45-yarder.

Bennett then forced a Mark Ingram fumble on the first play of the second quarter to set up a 15-yard touchdown run by Lynch to make it 13-0. And another Hauschka field goal then made it 16-0 at halftime.

That forced New Orleans, which came in committed to the run more than it had in the regular-season matchup, to begin altering its strategy.

The Saints moved at times, getting inside Seattle territory on five of its first six drives of the second half.

But New Orleans could score only two touchdowns, once failing on a fourth down and then seeing Graham miss a field goal from 48 yards with the score 16-8 and just 3:51 left in the game.

At that point, Seattle had just two first downs in the second half. Carroll said the Seahawks were careful in what they called in the third quarter when they were going into the wind.

"We didn't want to make crucial mistakes when we were backed up," Carroll said. "So we just played good grind-it-out football."

But facing a third-and-three at their own 45 and 2:57 left, the Seahawks decided to throw caution to all that wind blowing around. Wilson, seeing New Orleans ready to blitz, dropped back and threw 24 yards to Doug Baldwin, who was in man coverage down the sideline.

"It couldn't have been more clutch," Carroll said.

Lynch then busted free on a power running play the Seahawks had saved up for this week, throwing a stiff-arm on New Orleans cornerback Keenan Lewis as he ran into the end zone.

"Ah man, this feels awesome," said fullback Michael Robinson. He added, in reference to the NFC Championship Game against the 49ers: "But this don't mean nothing if we don't win next week."

don Mebane said. "Mike Bennett, he don't care, man. That's just how he plays. He plays hard, so hard, every game."

The defense also held Saints tight end Jimmy Graham, who got in at least two pre-game shouting matches with Seattle players, to just one catch for 8 yards.

Of the pregame jousting, Seattle safety Earl Thomas said: "Just some chatter. But you love those moments. I'm never going to forget those guys trying to run through our drills. But they don't understand what's coming."

Said Graham: "(Bruce Irvin) tried to disrespect me, and I'm not going to let anyone disrespect me. I don't want to talk about it."

And while the passing game struggled, Seattle rushed for 174 yards, averaging 5.0 yards a carry.

"This is exactly why you make a commitment to be a balanced offense and a balanced football team," Carroll said.

Marshawn Lynch put the game out of reach with 2:40 left in the fourth quarter on a 31-yard touchdown run, which he celebrated with tight end Zach Miller.

By John Lok / The Seattle Times

Richard Sherman was in the middle of the action during and after the NFC Championship Game, celebrating with ecstatic fans at CenturyLink Field after the game.

By John Lok / The Seattle Times

SEAHAWKS	49ERS

SUPER TIP!

Sherman's defensive play wins NFC, sets up a Super Bowl against Denver

By **BOB CONDOTTA** | *Seattle Times staff reporter*

It was frustrating. Then dizzying. Then nail-biting.

When it ended, though, there was simply celebrating as the Seattle Seahawks beat their rival San Francisco 49ers, 23-17, to advance to play the Denver Broncos in Super Bowl XLVIII, doing so to the delight of a CenturyLink Field record crowd of 68,454.

"It doesn't get any better," said Seattle quarterback Russell Wilson, who overcame a fumble on the first play of the game to lead Seattle back from an early 10-0 deficit, throwing the go-ahead touchdown on a 35-yard pass on fourth-and-seven to Jermaine Kearse with 13:44 left.

The victory wasn't sealed, however, until a Colin Kaepernick pass in the end zone intended for Michael Crabtree was tipped by Seattle's Richard

Player Of The Game

Yes, running back Marshawn Lynch finished with 109 yards rushing, the second consecutive playoff game in which he surpassed the century mark. But more important, he rumbled 40 yards for a touchdown that tied the score at 10 with 9:51 left in the third quarter and ignited the CenturyLink crowd.

Marshawn Lynch, who rushed for 33 yards in the first half, surpassed that on this 40-yard touchdown run in the third quarter that tied the score at 10.

By John Lok / The Seattle Times

The game featured wild momentum swings in the second half, including this 69-yard punt return by Doug Baldwin that set up a Seattle field goal that cut San Francisco's lead to 17-13.

By John Lok / The Seattle Times

Sherman into the hands of linebacker Malcolm Smith with 22 seconds left.

The play came on first down after San Francisco had driven from its own 22-yard line, seemingly poised to spoil the party.

Seahawks players, though, said they never doubted, remembering all the times this season when the NFL's No. 1-rated defense had come through when it mattered most.

"I thought he was going to pick it or tip it," said middle linebacker Bobby Wagner. "It was dumb (by Kaepernick). He didn't really throw it far enough to where the player could catch it, and you know we've got corners."

Indeed Seattle does, and Sherman let everyone know it afterward, giving a choke sign he said was meant for Kaepernick, and taunting Crabtree, who he later emphatically called in his postgame news conference "a mediocre receiver."

"When you try the best corner in the game with a mediocre receiver, that's what happens," Sherman said.

It didn't look good early, though, when Wilson fumbled on the first play from scrimmage, leading to a San Francisco field goal.

Kaepernick then used his running (he had 98 of his 130 yards in the first half) to set up a 1-yard touchdown run by Anthony Dixon.

A 51-yard Wilson to Doug Baldwin pass set up a Steven Hauschka 32-yard field goal that cut the lead to 10-3 at halftime. Still, there were nervous murmurs throughout the CenturyLink Field crowd at the half.

Coach Pete Carroll, though, said it was business as usual in the locker room, saying he reiterated a message from a meeting two days before the game, saying that the Seahawks "needed to take the next step, finish this football game playing better than they did longer. And our guys got that done."

A 40-yard touchdown run by Marshawn Lynch on Seattle's first second-half possession that tied the score got it started, kicking off a second half filled with big plays and momentum-changing moments on each side.

After a Kaepernick 26-yard touchdown pass to Anquan Boldin made it 17-10, a 69-yard kickoff return by Baldwin set up another Hauschka field goal (of 40 yards) to make it 17-13 entering the final quarter.

On its first possession of the fourth quarter, Seattle faced a fourth-and-seven at the 49ers 35, and a big decision — attempt a long field goal, or go for it?

Jermaine Kearse, left, and Russell Wilson celebrate Kearse's 35-yard touchdown reception that came on a fourth-down play and gave the Seahawks the lead for the first time early in the fourth quarter.

By John Lok / The Seattle Times

"It doesn't get any better," said quarterback Russell Wilson, embracing Seahawks coach Pete Carroll.

By Dean Rutz / The Seattle Times

Game statistics

San Francisco	3	7	7	0	17
Seattle	0	3	10	10	23

FIRST QUARTER

SF—FG Dawson 25, 12:45. Drive: 4 plays, 8 yards, 2:05.

SECOND QUARTER

SF—Dixon 1 run (Dawson kick), 10:03. Drive: 9 plays, 86 yards, 4:46.

Sea—FG Hauschka 32, 5:47. Drive: 9 plays, 62 yards, 4:16.

THIRD QUARTER

Sea—Lynch 40 run (Hauschka kick), 9:51. Drive: 4 plays, 60 yards, 2:15.

SF—Boldin 26 pass from Kaepernick (Dawson kick), 6:29. Drive: 6 plays, 83 yards, 3:22.

Sea—FG Hauschka 40, 3:55. Drive: 5 plays, 11 yards, 2:34.

FOURTH QUARTER

Sea—Kearse 35 pass from Wilson (Hauschka kick), 13:44. Drive: 8 plays, 62 yards, 4:03.

Sea—FG Hauschka 47, 3:37. Drive: 7 plays, 11 yards, 4:00.

A—68,454.

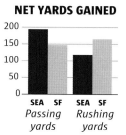

NET YARDS GAINED

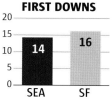

FIRST DOWNS

SEA 14   SF 16

■ 5 Rushing 7
■ 8 Passing 8
■ 1 Penalties 1

TIME OF POSSESSION

28:32 SF   31:28 SEA

Initially, the field goal team went out, with Wilson saying "I'm begging on the sidelines" to instead go for it. After a timeout, Carroll changed his mind. As San Francisco's Aldon Smith jumped offsides on a double-count by Wilson, Seattle changed its play on the fly, receivers running deep instead, knowing there was no risk to an interception.

"If they jumped offsides we were going to try to take a shot down field, and sure enough they did," Wilson said.

Wilson threw into the end zone where Kearse caught it in traffic, tumbling to the ground as he did.

Cliff Avril then forced a Kaepernick fumble that Seattle returned to the 6, and it looked like it might go from hard to easy quickly. Instead, a bad exchange between Wilson and Lynch led to a fumble on a fourth-and-goal from the 1.

Kaepernick was then intercepted by Kam Chancellor at the 40. But Seattle was held to a 47-yard Hauschka field goal that made it 23-17 with 3:37 remaining.

Seattle's defense had another opportunity to end it with 2:01 left when San Francisco had a fourth-and-two at its own 30. But Kaepernick hit Frank Gore for 17 yards, and then the 49ers began to move, eventually reaching the 18 with 30 seconds remaining.

Crabtree ended up matched up on Sherman, who said he'd had only one other pass thrown his way all day (a play on which he was called for holding).

"As soon as the ball went up in the air I knew we had a chance to make that play," Sherman said. "We stood up when it counted. None of us wanted to feel what we felt in Atlanta (when the Seahawks allowed a winning field goal in the final seconds of the playoffs last year) ever again."

Sherman said he intentionally tried to tip the ball high.

"I knew one of our guys would have a chance at it," he said.

That turned out to be Smith, who forced the 49ers' third turnover of the quarter and said: "I was just happy to be the guy to catch it. That's just the way our defense works."

Richard Sherman preserved the win with an acrobatic play in the end zone, tipping a pass intended for Michael Crabtree into the air before Malcolm Smith came down with the interception. "As soon as the ball went up in the air I knew we had a chance to make that play," Sherman said.

By Dean Rutz / The Seattle Times

A raucous crowd of 68,454, a CenturyLink record, watched the Seahawks rally from an early 10-0 deficit to knock off the 49ers and advance to the Super Bowl.

By Lindsey Wasson / The Seattle Times

Winning rituals

The methods might look strange, but many Seahawks diehards do all they can to help their team to a title

By JACK BROOM | *Seattle Times staff reporter*

Seahawks fans: Do you shave your head every weekend, like Lorin "Big Lo" Sandretzky of Burien?

Do you wear the same earrings, day and night, for months, like Shelley Anderson of Lake Stevens?

And when you're watching the Seahawks at home, and the other team has the ball, do you simply get up and leave the room, to keep them from scoring, like Eva Froemke of Ritzville?

No? Neither do we. But maybe we should.

While Sandretzky, Anderson and Froemke have been doing their thing for the past few months, the Seahawks have marched to an impressive record.

Skeptics might see little connection between sports fans' quirky habits and their teams' success, but don't tell that to Sandretzky.

He's been going to Seahawks games 28 years, but only this year went to the shaved-head look.

"When you do something and your team's winning, you keep doing it," Sandretzky said.

During the season, legions of Seahawks fans ate their special foods, drank their special drinks, wore their special attire — some even timed moments of romantic intimacy.

Sound crazy? Not to Eric Hamerman.

"They're doing what they can to help the team," said Hamerman, an assistant marketing professor at Tulane University.

Hamerman and Columbia University business professor Gita Johar last spring published a paper on "conditioned superstitions."

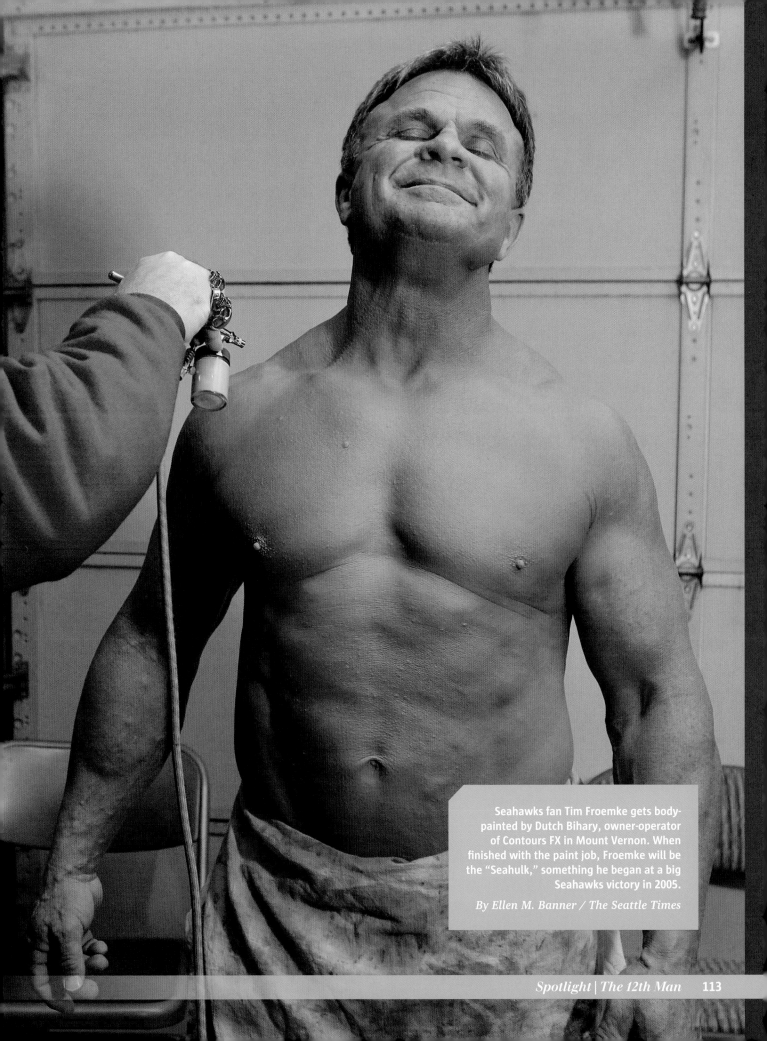

Seahawks fan Tim Froemke gets body-painted by Dutch Bihary, owner-operator of Contours FX in Mount Vernon. When finished with the paint job, Froemke will be the "Seahulk," something he began at a big Seahawks victory in 2005.

By Ellen M. Banner / The Seattle Times

Those are the beliefs that give sports fans the sense that something they do will help their favorite team's chances — even though there may be no apparent, logical connection.

"If I really want to control the outcome and I don't feel like I can, in any sort of rational way, then I'm more likely to reach for an irrational way," Hamerman said.

And if that irrational way "works," it can become an instant habit, cemented in place by each subsequent success.

Even a setback won't necessarily prompt fans to change what they consider a lucky habit. "If it doesn't work every time, they still might think it improves their chances," Hamerman said.

If the football gods are seeking a certain behavior from Seahawks fans, it's hard to tell what that is.

Like, what's their position on alcohol?

Sandy Snider, of Tacoma, says the Seahawks do better when she has a Bloody Mary before the game, either at a tailgate party outside CenturyLink Field or at home in front of the TV.

But Eddie Perdomo, of Monroe, says he helps the Hawks by abstaining from alcohol during football season. At one point last year, he allowed himself just a single shot, and the Seahawks lost their next game.

And what are fans supposed to eat?

It's got to be hot dogs for Jeff Mayhew, of Seattle, and his wife. They've had hot dogs before just about every game for the last couple of years. But when they flew to Atlanta for a playoff game in January, they were unable to find a hot-dog vendor outside the Georgia Dome. And the Seahawks lost, 30-28.

But wait a minute. Veronica Santiago, also from Seattle, says she and her husband used to eat hot dogs before every game but switched to tacos at a game against Arizona last December.

And they must have been some damn fine tacos, judging from the "results" on the field: Seahawks 58, Cardinals 0.

Seahawks fans wear all manner of "lucky" apparel, from furry boots to blue-and-green underwear to replica jerseys from players who've been gone from the team for decades.

A peek into the stands at CenturyLink Field reveals that "12th Man" jerseys and those for current Seahawks players are the go-to garments.

Some fans go home and wash their jerseys, so they'll be spotless for the next encounter. But others wear the same jersey all season without laundering it, to avoid rinsing away its precious powers.

And each group can claim — this year, anyway — that what they're doing is working.

Anderson, the Lake Stevens woman wearing Seahawks hoop earrings around the clock, has some pretty strong evidence of their power:

In December, one fell out and she was unable to find it. And while it was missing, the Seahawks lost to the 49ers, 19-17.

But a few days later, she found it, in time to watch the Seahawks' 23-0 victory over the New York Giants.

Jimbo "Cowbell Dude" Sabado, of Shoreline, has noticed that the Seahawks do better when he and his fianceé start the day with, uh, let's say a tender moment — and he says he's heard something similar from other fans.

His nickname comes from bringing his cowbell to the game, which stadium workers now prohibit. But the name has stuck.

Not all of the Seahawks fans' unusual practices, rituals and traditions are based on superstition.

Take that of Froemke's husband, Tim, as an example.

Starting with the Seahawks' victory at the NFC Championship Game in 2005, he has had his upper body painted green before certain home games to portray the Seahulk.

During the game, he urges fans around him to make as much noise as possible, especially when the visiting team is trying to call a play.

And by now, the whole NFL-watching world knows that the power of the 12th Man to rattle opponents at CenturyLink Field isn't superstition. It's fact.

Seahawks fans might be paying more attention to their habits this season because they're working so well.

But fans and superstitions have always gone hand in glove, said Mark Tye Turner, who recounts his own history as a Seahawks fan in his 2009 book, "Notes from a 12 Man."

Turner, a fan since the team's 1976 debut, said the most painful games are the close losses.

"They allow you to think you had some control over the situation," he wrote. "If only you had sat in a different chair or wore a different shirt, the outcome would have been more favorable.

"It's ridiculous," he wrote, "but sports fandom rarely operates logically."

Tim "Seahulk" Froemke (back row, second from left) is surrounded by other Seahawks fans who had gathered at a home in Bellevue to watch a road game on TV.

By Ellen M. Banner / The Seattle Times

BOOM TOWN

*Defense, special teams lead
Seahawks to Super romp*

By **BOB CONDOTTA** | *Seattle Times staff reporter*

They shut down Peyton Manning and shut up their critics.

And then, in the happy celebration of the Seahawks' first Super Bowl title in their 38-year history, defensive end Red Bryant stood up in the locker room and issued a challenge to everyone within earshot.

"This team has got to go down as one of the best defenses of all time," Bryant yelled after Seattle's 43-8 victory over the Denver Broncos at MetLife Stadium in East Rutherford, N.J. "It's got to. And the best thing about it is they called us misfits, overachievers, said that nobody wanted us. But now we're the best."

That they are, this merry collection of players, many of whom were low-round draft choices and undrafted free agents and now they can call them-

Player Of The Game

Malcolm Smith became the third linebacker to win Super Bowl MVP honors by returning an interception 69 yards for a touchdown that gave the Seahawks a 22-0 lead with 3:21 left in the first half and also recovering a fumble in the third quarter. Smith is the eighth defensive player overall to be Super Bowl MVP (Randy White and Harvey Martin shared the award in 1978).

Earl Thomas, left, and Richard Sherman, center, made sure nothing came easy for Demaryius Thomas and the Broncos' offense. Sherman suffered a high ankle sprain on this fourth-quarter play and missed the rest of the game.

By John Lok / The Seattle Times

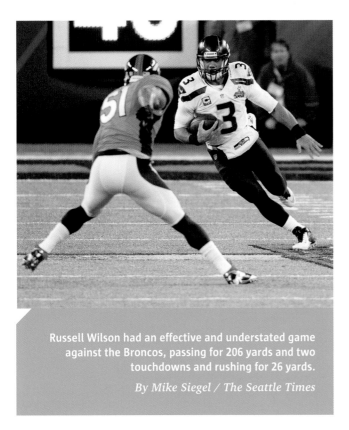

Russell Wilson had an effective and understated game against the Broncos, passing for 206 yards and two touchdowns and rushing for 26 yards.

By Mike Siegel / The Seattle Times

Game statistics

Seattle	8	14	14	7	— 43
Denver	0	0	8	0	— 8

FIRST QUARTER

Sea—Avril safety, 14:48.

Sea—FG Hauschka 31, 10:21. Drive: 9 plays, 51 yards, 4:27.

Sea—FG Hauschka 33, 2:16. Drive: 13 plays, 58 yards, 6:15.

SECOND QUARTER

Sea—Lynch 1 run (Hauschka kick), 12:00. Drive: 7 plays, 37 yards, 3:59.

Sea—Smith 69 interception return (Hauschka kick), 3:21.

THIRD QUARTER

Sea—Harvin 87 kickoff return (Hauschka kick), 14:48.

Sea—Kearse 23 pass from Wilson (Hauschka kick), 2:58. Drive: 6 plays, 58 yards, 2:57.

Den—D.Thomas 14 pass from Manning (Welker pass from Manning), :00. Drive: 6 plays, 80 yards, 2:58.

FOURTH QUARTER

Sea—Baldwin 10 pass from Wilson (Hauschka kick), 11:45. Drive: 5 plays, 65 yards, 3:15.

A—82,529.

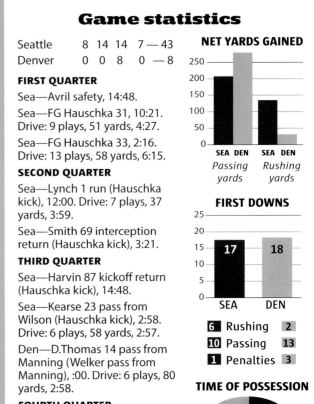

NET YARDS GAINED

FIRST DOWNS

SEA 17 DEN 18

6	Rushing	2
10	Passing	13
1	Penalties	3

TIME OF POSSESSION

28:07 DEN 31:53 SEA

selves the best in the world.

They dominated on defense, matching Denver's record-setting offense on their own, 8-8, and holding the Broncos scoreless until the last play of the third quarter. Some Seattle players were disappointed they didn't pitch the first shutout in Super Bowl history.

The Seahawks were opportunistic on offense, scoring touchdowns after two Denver turnovers, taking shots in the passing game when they were there, more often than not converting. Russell Wilson threw two touchdown passes in a typically understated performance, going 18 for 25 for 206 yards.

And Seattle was flashy on special teams, with Percy Harvin's 87-yard kickoff return to start the second half putting it up 29-0, essentially sealing the deal.

And if anyone else was surprised it was so easy, the Seahawks weren't, living up to every expectation they had brazenly heaped on themselves.

"I'm trying to be nice about it," said receiver Golden Tate, "but we know that we have a special group of guys. … At the end of the day we want

to play us, and do us, and if the opposition shows up to play it'll be a good game. If not, we will run you out of the stadium. And there's not a better stage to do this on. A lot of people had the Broncos dominating us and that wasn't the case."

And when it was over, Seattle had its first championship in one of the four major professional sports leagues since the now-departed SuperSonics captured the NBA title in 1979.

It came in the Seahawks' second Super Bowl appearance after having lost to Pittsburgh 21-10 in 2006. The victory came in the fourth year in Seattle for coach Pete Carroll, hired after the 2009 season to revive a team that had won just nine games the previous two years.

"It played out the way we wanted it to play out," said Carroll, who became just the third coach to win both a college national title and a Super Bowl. The others are Jimmy Johnson (Miami, Dallas Cowboys) and Barry Switzer (Oklahoma, Dallas Cowboys). "All phases contributed. It was not re-

Linebacker Malcolm Smith took an interception 69 yards for a touchdown in the second quarter to blow the game open. Smith recovered a fumble in the third quarter and was named the game's most valuable player.

By John Lok / The Seattle Times

ally even a question in our mind that we wouldn't perform like this."

The game turned Seattle's way from the start, as a mistimed snap on Denver's first offensive play led to a Seahawks safety, credited to Cliff Avril, just 12 seconds into the game — the fastest score in Super Bowl history.

After two Seattle field goals came a pair of backbreakers forced by the Seattle defense.

Late in the first quarter, Manning threw a wobbly pass over the middle under heavy pressure into the hands of Seattle safety Kam Chancellor.

That led to a 1-yard-touchdown run by Mar-

shawn Lynch that put Seattle ahead 15-0 with exactly 12 minutes remaining in the second quarter.

At that point, Seattle had a 165-11 edge in yards and a 9-0 edge in first downs against a Denver offense that had scored a record 606 points this season.

A series later, Manning was hit by Avril as he

Kam Chancellor celebrates his first-quarter interception that led to Marshawn Lynch's 1-yard touchdown run. The Seahawks intercepted two passes and forced four turnovers.

By John Lok / The Seattle Times

Doug Baldwin capped the Seahawks' scoring on this 10-yard touchdown catch early in the fourth quarter.

By John Lok / The Seattle Times

threw, with the ball falling into the hands of linebacker Malcolm Smith, who had an easy path to a 69-yard touchdown to make it 22-0 with 3:21 left in the first half. The play helped land Smith honors as the game's most valuable player after also recovering a fumble in the third quarter.

Seattle defensive coordinator Dan Quinn said the Seahawks didn't really do anything different, other than play more nickel against Denver's one-back offense, which also meant playing more man coverage.

"I knew we'd play well tonight," Quinn said. "We really held them in high regard but at the same time we wanted them to deal with us, too, and I think that oftentimes gets overlooked."

And just in case there were any questions Seattle might get fat and happy with the halftime lead, Harvin's kickoff return — he scored with 12 seconds gone in the half — answered them. The second half became an extended Seattle sideline party.

The Seahawks had been as far as a conference title game just twice since entering the NFL in 1976.

But that history didn't daunt this Seahawks team, which began to find itself last season when it advanced to the divisional playoff round before losing a heartbreaker at Atlanta.

The Seahawks vowed not to let that happen again, and talked openly of getting to, and winning, the Super Bowl.

"To be honest with you, I think a lot of the players on the team expected it to be a dominating win," said receiver Doug Baldwin, who led the Seahawks with 66 yards and scored a touchdown and said afterward the team has already set its sights on winning another to cement itself as one of the greatest teams ever.

But Bryant, one of just four players left from the pre-Carroll days, understood how special the moment was.

"I know how fortunate I am to be in this moment and I don't take it for granted," he said. "This is a team that whenever you think about the Seattle Seahawks, you are going to think about this team. You are going to think about this win."

Quarterback Peyton Manning set a Super Bowl record with 34 completions, but he was harassed by Bobby Wagner, top, and Cliff Avril, bottom, on this play.

By Mike Siegel / The Seattle Times

Percy Harvin was off and running in the first half for the Seahawks, rushing for 45 yards on two carries. He later returned the second-half kickoff 87 yards for a touchdown to put the game out of reach.

By Dean Rutz / The Seattle Times

Ball Hawks

Defense shows how great it can be

By **LARRY STONE** | *Seattle Times columnist*

Pete Carroll allowed himself a champion's laugh, his hair still damp from the Gatorade bath, and the glow of a dream fulfilled exuding from every pore.

"All those people who say that defense wins championships can gloat for a while," he said. "That's exactly what we did."

Give due praise, of course, to Russell Wilson's poise beyond his years, and Marshawn Lynch's relentless running.

Duly note the belated contribution by the blur that is Percy Harvin, and allow the rest of the Seahawks' not-so-pedestrian receiving corps the last laugh they richly deserve.

But make no mistake about it: The Seahawks — the Super Bowl champion Seahawks — are a team built on defense, and predicated on defense. Their stunning 43-8 win over Denver was validation not only of that unit, but of an entire philosophy of team-building.

The outcome Sunday was so unambiguous, so glaringly, in-your-face decisive, that it not-so-subtly altered the plot line of the entire Super Bowl buildup. All week, the game was billed as a referendum on Peyton Manning's legacy. Instead, it turned into a mandate on the historic nature of Seattle's defense.

To defensive lineman Michael Bennett, the conclusion was obvious.

"I told you, we're the best defense ever," he said. "We could have played anyone today and did the same thing."

The Seahawks played a Broncos offense that had scored the most points in NFL history, led by a future Hall of Fame quarterback in Manning who had thrown for the most yards and touchdowns ever. And Seattle made the whole lot of them look, well, pedestrian.

Manning set a Super Bowl record with 34 completions, but it was an empty achievement, like scoring 40 points in a blowout basketball loss or hitting a three-run homer when down 10-0 in the ninth. The Seahawks were ready for everything Manning threw at them, including his vaunted signal-calling at the line of scrimmage.

Jermaine Kearse, center, celebrates with Zach Miller, left, and Derrick Coleman, right, after Kearse scored on a 23-yard touchdown pass in the third quarter that put the Seahawks ahead, 36-0.

By John Lok / The Seattle Times

The Seahawks matched him audible for audible. When Manning threw out an "Omaha" or other code word, middle linebacker Bobby Wagner nodded and barked out some signals of his own — admitting later that a few were bogus words just designed to confuse the Broncos.

"You've got to understand, some of his calls are fake, too," Wagner said. "He's not checking every single play. We felt we had a good pickup from watching on film, when he was going to check and when he wasn't. We were just on. We felt we had the offense down pat. We definitely came ready for Peyton."

When asked how in the world the Seahawks could shut down an offense that had steamrolled all comers, Wagner said with a shrug: "They haven't played a defense like ours. We watch a lot of film, and defenses (they faced) weren't as fast and physical as ours."

"The only way we can say we're the best defense is to take down the best offense. And we did that. I defi-

nitely feel we're up there. We went against a legend, a guy who will definitely go into the Hall of Fame as soon as he retires. Who knows? We have to do a lot more. If we really want to be the best, we've got to keep it going for longer than just a year."

But that's a quest for another day. On this glorious evening, the Seahawks were savoring a defensive performance that truly accentuated the synergy of the unit. The pass rush was in sync with the coverage, causing Manning discomfort in the pocket at the same time he was limited to innocuously short passes.

Meanwhile, the Seahawks were hitting the Broncos with such ferocity that it seemed to deflate their will. And that started on Denver's first possession after the game-opening safety, when Kam Chancellor dropped Demaryius Thomas with a thunderous hit.

"That definitely set the tone," Chancellor said.

In the Super Bowl, they competed at the highest level on the biggest stage, and put themselves on the map with the greatest defenses ever.

"It's all about making history," safety Earl Thomas said.

In this game, the Seahawks 'D' had earned the right to gloat.

Seahawks fans were well represented at MetLife Stadium during the Super Bowl. Here, Aaron Underseth, left, hugs James Sense as Sense's wife, Michelle, celebrates during the second quarter.

By Genevieve Alvarez / The Seattle Times

Seahawks playoff roster

OFFENSE

P	#	Name	Ht	Wt
QB	3	Russell Wilson	5-11	206
	7	Tarvaris Jackson	6-2	225
RB	22	Robert Turbin	5-10	222
	24	Marshawn Lynch	5-11	215
	40	Derrick Coleman	6-0	233
	26	Michael Robinson	6-1	240
	33	Christine Michael	5-10	221
TE	82	Luke Willson	6-5	252
	86	Zach Miller	6-5	255
	87	Kellen Davis	6-7	265
WR	15	Jermaine Kearse	6-1	209
	81	Golden Tate	5-10	202
	11	Percy Harvin	5-11	184
	19	Bryan Walters	6-0	190
	83	Ricardo Lockette	6-2	211
	89	Doug Baldwin	5-10	189
G	64	J.R. Sweezy	6-5	298
	67	Paul McQuistan	6-6	315
	73	Michael Bowie	6-4	332
	77	James Carpenter	6-5	321
T	68	Breno Giacomini	6-7	318
	74	Caylin Hauptmann	6-3	300
	76	Russell Okung	6-5	310
	78	Alvin Bailey	6-3	320
C	49	Clint Gresham	6-3	240
	60	Max Unger	6-5	305
	61	Lemuel Jeanpierre	6-3	301
K	4	Steven Hauschka	6-4	210

DEFENSE

P	#	Name	Ht	Wt
DE	56	Cliff Avril	6-3	260
	72	Michael Bennett	6-4	274
	79	Red Bryant	6-4	323
	91	Chris Clemons	6-3	254
	95	Benson Mayowa	6-3	252
DT	92	Brandon Mebane	6-1	311
	69	Clinton McDonald	6-2	297
	97	Jordan Hill	6-1	303
	99	Tony McDaniel	6-7	305
LB	55	Heath Farwell	6-0	235
	50	K.J. Wright	6-4	246
	51	Bruce Irvin	6-3	248
	53	Malcolm Smith	6-0	226
	54	Bobby Wagner	6-0	241
	57	Mike Morgan	6-3	226
	93	O'Brien Schofield	6-3	242
S	29	Earl Thomas	5-10	202
	31	Kam Chancellor	6-3	232
	42	Chris Maragos	5-10	200
CB	20	Jeremy Lane	6-0	190
	25	Richard Sherman	6-3	195
	28	Walter Thurmond	5-11	190
	35	DeShawn Shead	6-2	220
	41	Byron Maxwell	6-1	207
P	9	Jon Ryan	6-0	217

ILLUSTRATION BY DAVID MILLER / THE SEATTLE TIMES